TOWARD A GEOGRAPHY OF PRICE

TOWARD A GEOGRAPHY OF PRICE

A STUDY IN GEO-ECONOMETRICS

by William Warntz
Research Associate
The American Geographical Society, New York

PHILADELPHIA
UNIVERSITY OF PENNSYLVANIA PRESS

PUBLISHED IN GREAT BRITAIN, INDIA, AND PAKISTAN
BY THE OXFORD UNIVERSITY PRESS
LONDON, BOMBAY, AND KARACHI

LIBRARY OF CONGRESS CATALOGUE CARD NUMBER: 57–7220

PRINTED AND BOUND IN ENGLAND
BY W. & J. MACKAY & CO. LTD, CHATHAM

Preface

THIS work represents a fusion of some of the major interests of the author during the seven years he was on the faculty of the Wharton School of Finance and Commerce of the University of Pennsylvania. Combined are ideas and methods from Geography, Economics, and Statistics, but throughout the study the preoccupation of the Geographer with spatial relationships prevails.

It is hoped that the laborious winnowing has produced at least a small grain that is worthwhile. If this be the case, then there are many who can lay claim to a share of the credit. Dr. Lester E. Klimm, Professor of Geography at the University of Pennsylvania, was in close association with the author throughout the entire period of the study. In addition to furnishing many helpful suggestions, Dr. Klimm demonstrated a patience and forbearance with what at times must have been a "trying young man" far beyond the requirements of his office.

Dr. John Q. Stewart, Professor of Astronomical Physics at Princeton University and Chairman of the Committee on Social Physics, whose considerable writings on "population potential" furnished the first basic ideas from which this study subsequently developed, encouraged the author considerably from time to time, and offered countless invaluable criticisms during the many occasions when he graciously entertained the author at Princeton. It is the author's hope that Professor Stewart will accept this work as an interest payment on the astronomical academic debt owed him by the author.

Others at the University of Pennsylvania who gave freely of their time and advice include Dr. R. T. Bowman, Economics, and Dr. E. D. Burdick of the Statistics Department.

To all these persons and the many more who were kind enough to offer suggestions, the author is indebted and takes this opportunity to express his gratitude. Special thanks are owed to Miss Elizabeth Hope, who proofread and typed the final manuscript.

In a special category, of course, is my wife who performed the function of "handy man" throughout the period of the study. She cheerfully assisted with many tasks, not the least appreciated of which was her "making tea" at any hour of the night. She deserves a special kind of gratitude I find difficult to express. This occasion is taken to continue my expression of gratefulness to her.

WILLIAM WARNTZ

CONTENTS

TABLES AND FIGURES

TABLES

FIGURES

TOWARD A GEOGRAPHY OF PRICE

1

Considerations of the Dimensions of Society with Special Reference to Economic Activity

A. Introduction

"GEOGRAPHY and history fill up the entire circumference of our perceptions: geography that of space, history that of time."[1]

Events happen at times and at places; and the nature of the event itself, its magnitude, the place, and the time of its occurrence constitute the circumstances of its reality.

Space and time have long been recognized by physical scientists to be of the utmost significance. John Q. Stewart, an Associate Professor of Astronomical Physics at Princeton University, is of the opinion that it was by grasping the fundamental usefulness of distance and time for physical thought that Galileo succeeded in starting Physics as an operational science.[2]

Stewart further adds that although Galileo recognized the usefulness of distance and time in the analysis of physical phenomena, he did not fully understand what he was doing. It was actually the beginning of the nineteenth century that witnessed the emergence of dimensional analysis in the physical sciences. The French mathematician and physicist J. B. J. Fourier could be considered as

[1] A statement attributed to Immanuel Kant about 1759 and quoted in *Immanuel Kant's Physische Geographie*, edited by F. T. Rink (Königsberg, 1802), I.

[2] So stated by Dr. Stewart to the author during a discussion at Princeton, New Jersey, March 3, 1955.

the leader of the school that finally recognized the role of physical dimensions, according to Stewart.

A drop of rain falls; a price is paid for a bushel of wheat. We have come arbitrarily to classify the former as a physical phenomenon and the latter as an economic phenomenon. Yet, both have in common in the reality of their occurrence the facts that they happen at a time and at a place. The fact that human attitudes and dispositions are involved in the second phenomenon and not in the first does not mean that the second one does not have measurable physical dimensions. But, early in the history of the social sciences, there was a strong tendency to place complete emphasis upon the so-called human aspects of economic phenomena without regard to the physical dimensions of the data save for those quantities relating to magnitude. That this was the case and that only now are the full dimensions of economic activity being reckoned with will be pointed out in the subsequent portions of this chapter.

B. *To the End of the Nineteenth Century*

Following the Renaissance and the subsequent social, political, religious, agricultural, industrial, and accompanying revolutions, there emerged also in Europe a revolution in thought and the development of the scientific method. The new scientists who concerned themselves with physical phenomena recognized, as indicated above, the significance of all the dimensions of their data, while the social scientists as a group did not. In fact, whenever social data were subjected to dimensional analysis, it was frequently by physical scientists who crossed recognized boundaries between disciplines. Particular instances of this will be discussed subsequently.

The Classical School of Economics developed a system

of economic thought which was conceived by Adam Smith toward the end of the eighteenth century and which grew into a body of doctrine under the impetus of such men as Malthus and Ricardo. In mid-nineteenth century John Stuart Mill formalized and synthesized the body of thought into a single statement of the doctrines of Classical Economics.[3]

But the shortcomings of the system were many and the literature of later periods is filled with attacks on what, in hindsight, seem to be obvious defects.

Walter Isard, then of the Massachusetts Institute of Technology, in speaking of later adherents to this Classical School of Economics said that they created a "wonderland of no dimensions."[4] And it was this failure of the Classicists in particular and social scientists in general to recognize the need for dimensional analysis that is surprising when it is realized that the physical scientists of the new order were doing so.

However, as more and more studies of economic phenomena were made, the Economists gradually came to realize that certain data previously assumed to be homogeneous really were not because they were distributed through time. An important deviation from Classical thought appeared among the writers of what might be called the Historical School of Economic Thought.[5]

[3] J. S. Mill, *Principles of Political Economy* (London: 1848).

[4] W. Isard, "The General Theory of Location and Space-Economy," *Quarterly Journal of Economics*, LXIII (1949), 477.

[5] Other reactions after mid-nineteenth century to Classical thought were propounded by the Austrian Marginalists, the Optimists, the Nationalists, the Idealists, the Socialists, the Neoclassicists, the Institutionalists, *et al.* Each is of tremendous significance and interest. They share alike the fact that their objections were primarily based on the Classical School's failure to recognize some aspect of reality—reality, that is, in the minds of the objectors. As important as they are, separate consideration of these schools lies beyond the scope of this study.

Of course it would be naive to assume that recognition of time significance was the only contribution of the Historical School. The term "historical" refers to but one aspect of this new conception of economic activity. The school also stressed the need for examining social reality as a whole, for giving economic study greater empirical content, for insistence upon verification of theory in light of quantitative data, and for the creation of social justice through economic reforms by recourse to social legislation.

Although the Historical School had some adherents in Britain, such as Ingram, Leslie, Bagehot, and the first Toynbee, its origin and development occurred on the continent, primarily in Germany, where such men as Kneis, Hildebrand, Roscher, Schmoller, and others followed the early lead of Mueller and List. Perhaps it was Schmoller who most succinctly stated the primary method of the Historical School when he stated that it was the aim of Economic History simply to arrange systematically in time the occurrences of the past, utilizing this as a means to a narration and explanation of the facts.[6]

Where among the critics of Classical Economics were those who had come to realize that certain data assumed to be homogeneous really were not, because they were distributed spatially, that is, across the earth's surface? Who insisted upon the systematic arrangement of data in terms of spatial or areal distribution, using this as a means to narration and explanation of the facts? Who asked if *where* an event occurred was economically significant? In effect then, where was the school of economic thought that could be called Economic Geography? As late as the latter half of the nineteenth century neither the Economists nor the Geographers constituted such a school of thought.

[6] G. V. Schmoller, *Political Economy and its Method* (Berlin, 1894).

However, certain isolated individuals had concerned themselves with spatial relationships. As early as the seventeenth century the philosopher Gottfried von Leibniz foresaw a generalized logic which would translate through analogy the concepts and relationships of one field into those of another by means of vocabulary equivalences.[7] Leibniz saw no distinction between physical and social phenomena in terms of their suitability to time-space analysis.

The founder of the French Philosophical School of Positivism, Auguste Comte, recognized early in the nineteenth century the significance of physical factors in social processes and expressed the necessity of appreciating the "coexistence and succession in time and space" of all phenomena. In 1830 Comte used the term "Social Physics" as synonymous with a possible interpretation of society using a dimensional analysis.[8] However, he did not attempt such an analysis.

In 1836 the remarkable Belgian astronomer, Adolphe Quetelet, "crossed" disciplinary boundaries and suggested the application of mathematical methods to the increasing volume of social statistics. In addition to advocating the use of a dimensional analysis, Quetelet popularized the concept of the "average man," being careful also to warn of the limitations of this measure. The best expression of this physical scientist's attitudes toward a projected study of social phenomena can be found in his work, *Sur l'homme* (Brussels, 1836). Quetelet also used the term "Social Physics," apparently independently of Comte.

In 1858, Philadelphia publisher Henry C. Carey,

[7] The contribution of Leibniz is discussed by John Q. Stewart in "The Development of Social Physics," *American Journal of Physics*, XVIII, No. 5 (1950), 241.

[8] See especially Harriet Martineau, *The Philosophy of Auguste Comte* (London, 1853).

controversial but original in his attitudes, published his own three-volume *Principles of Social Science.* Best remembered for his attacks upon the pessimistic conclusions of the Classical School, he is mentioned here primarily because he emphasized numbers of people and their distances apart as social factors of considerable importance. He suggested that people exert an influence on other people and that this influence varies directly with the size of the population exerting the influence and inversely with distance. He likened this influence to a "gravitation" effect.[9] Carey thereby anticipated the concept of "Population Potential" developed by Dr. John Q. Stewart and discussed in Chapter II of this study.

If Carey was one of the very few Economists to turn his attention to spatial distribution of economic phenomena, so also was J. H. von Thünen. In his *Isolated State,*[10] von Thünen made a most significant contribution when he demonstrated that even if all land were of uniform quality (i.e., of similar site characteristics), patterns of differential land use and differential economic rent would develop, based on relative position alone. To this day von Thünen's scheme of agriculture in concentric zones around population concentrations fairly adequately described reality even with differences in terrain, the inequality of resource distribution, diversification on individual farms, legislation, and the like influencing land utilization.

In 1872 J. E. Hilgard, a civil engineer and geodesist in the employ of the United States Coast and Geodetic Survey, offered a short article entitled "The Advance of

[9] H. C. Carey, *Principles of Social Science,* Vol. I (Philadelphia, 1858), p. 42. "Man tends of necessity to gravitate toward his fellow man. . . . Gravitation is here, as everywhere else in the material world, in the direct ratio of the mass and the inverse one of the distance."

[10] J. H. von Thünen, *Der Isolierte Staat in Beziehung auf Landwirthschaft und National Ökonomie,* 3 vols. (Hamburg, 1826–1863).

Population in the United States," which appeared in a popular magazine of the day.[11] Hilgard used the methods known for calculating the center of gravity of mass distributed on a plane and calculated a center of gravity for the population of the United States. He also described the previous westward movement of this point and made a forecast of future movement, which to this date has been fairly accurate.

Although other centroids can be calculated that are more useful for certain problems the Bureau of the Census still calculates and gives widespread publicity to the center of gravity of population of the United States, having unfortunately once ascribed attributes to it that it does not possess.

Another German scholar, Launhardt, an Economist, turned his attention to spatial analysis and produced a penetrating analysis of the location of specific manufacturing industries in terms of transport costs, market areas, and raw material sources. He failed, however, to produce a general theory of location of economic activity. His principal work[12] in 1882 was the first attempt to develop a locational theory.

Three years later, Ravenstein developed empirical evidence of an inverse distance relationship in social phenomena.[13] He investigated the distances traveled by migrants and demonstrated with statistical material that the number moving into a center from a given point varies inversely with the distance between the points and directly with the size of the populations.

[11] J. E. Hilgard, "The Advance of Population in the United States," *Scribner's Monthly*, IV (1872), 214.

[12] W. Launhardt, "Die Bestimmung des zweckmässigsten Standortes einer gewerblichen Anlage," *Zeitschrift des Vereins deutscher Ingenieure*, XXVI, No. 3 (1882).

[13] E. G. Ravenstein, "The Laws of Migration," *Journal of the Royal Statistical Society*, XLVIII (1805), 167–227.

Lester F. Ward, a paleobotanist who turned his attention to sociology, is quoted by Stewart as writing near the end of the last century that:

> . . . three ultimate elements in mechanical theory are mass, space, and time. The theory of units is applicable to every true science in proportion as it can be reduced to exact measurement. In mechanics, astronomy, and physics the phenomena can, for the most part, be thus reduced; but in the more complex sciences, at least in their present state, this can be done only to a limited extent.[14]

Ward anticipated a dimensional analysis of social phenomena.

In the same article Stewart comments on the writings of Emile Durkheim in France, who concerned himself with populations and their distances apart in a manner reminiscent of the work of Carey thirty years earlier.

And finally, around the end of the century the brilliant Russian chemist, Dimitri Ivanovich Mendeleyev, spent the last few years of his life examining social data.[15] He calculated a center of gravity of population for Russia from the census of 1897.

The nineteenth century, then, was one in which the dimensional analysis of data in the physical sciences was instituted with a subsequent rigorous mathematical development. On the other hand, economic science, as developed by the Classical School during the first half of the century, was based on abstract logical deductions which, unfortunately, ignored the reality of the time and space distributions of economic phenomena.

[14] Quoted by J. Q. Stewart in "A Basis for Social Physics," *Impact*, III, No. 2 (1952), 112.

[15] D. I. Mendeleyev, *K Poznaniyu Rossii* (Information on Russia), 3rd ed. (St. Petersburg, 1906).

However, by mid-nineteenth century a group of men representing the historical approach to economics, and conveniently classified as Economic Historians, began to attack the Classical School and insist upon the recognition of time, development and growth, and change as normal occurrences. No longer could they approve a theory which admitted of time as simply a disturbing friction and not as an inescapable attribute of the occurrence of all phenomena.

Hence, the creation by the Economic Historians of theories including time as an internal part and necessary to the completeness of the whole represents a major attempt by Economists to make economics more than an exercise in logic. Interest rate and business cycle theories were subsequently developed as well. But distance and space were still considered to be external frictions (if they were considered at all) by the vast majority of Economists and no attempt was made to make distance or space integral parts of existing theory except for the contributions of von Thünen, Carey, and Launhardt.

Note again, however, that there were scholars interested in space aspects of society and economic activity. However, these investigations in many instances were carried on by physical scientists "crossing" disciplinary boundaries.

What of the Geographers of the nineteenth century?

"Geography has its roots in Classical Antiquity, but its development as a modern discipline crystallized in Europe, and primarily in Germany, during the period 1750 to 1900."[16]

In the nineteenth century two different methods of approach developed: one, the systematic studies concentrating on areal difference of specific elements over the

[16] R. Hartshorne, "The Nature of Geography," *Annals of the Association of American Geographers*, XXIX, Nos. 3 and 4 (1939), 35.

whole earth; the other, regional studies of many elements in a specific area.

In addition to this "dualism," another existed in the question as to whether Geography should be concerned with physical or with human phenomena. A too-simple, but convenient, classification of the existing schools of thought concerning the two "dualisms" would be into those who followed Baron Alexander von Humboldt and placed their emphasis upon systematic and physical geography and those who patterned themselves after Karl Ritter and were more interested in regional and human geography.

Following the death of both men in 1859, the Ritterian influence persisted for a time because he had been a university professor who left students behind. But by the end of the century geographic thought had become concentrated on the relationship (considered to be one largely of determinism) between man and his physical environment (with landforms being the element of the physical environment most often utilized to account for man's activities).

Although Geographers collected, classified, and systematized their data in terms of spatial distribution, it is safe to conclude that they were not especially interested in economic activity as such, cared little for economic theory, and certainly made little attempt to develop a theory of economic activity recognizing the significance of space and distance such as the Economic Historians had developed with time.

Geographical description of (i.e., assigning location to) economic activity alone does not constitute spatial analysis of economic activity and in the nineteenth century the paths of geographers and economists rarely crossed.

C. Since 1900

The nineteenth century, then, can be characterized as one in which, during the first half, physical scientists carried out dimensional analysis while social scientists did not. During the second half the physical scientists developed rigorous mathematical concepts while the social scientists did begin to explore the possibilities of dimensional analysis with regard to time but still continued largely to overlook the significance of spatial distribution.

However, the twentieth century has produced an imposing mass of empirical findings on distance and spatial relationships in social phenomena. The beginning of the development of a general theory of the space economy, emphasizing both location and an expanded general equilibrium price theory including spatial relationships, has also taken place in this century. But Isard has said that it is the impressive mass of empirical findings "that focuses attention upon a gross inadequacy of existing economic theory: its failure to develop (separate) concepts for spatial analysis."[17]

Isard has contributed many significant journal articles including "The General Theory of Location and Space-Economy."[18] In this particular article, Isard does not actually contribute to theory, but instead is concerned with the need for a space theory. The article also is extremely useful in that it contains a survey of relatively recent attempts to create a general location theory. This

[17] W. Isard, "Distance Inputs and the Space Economy, Part I: The Conceptual Framework," *The Quarterly Journal of Economics*, LXV (1951), 181.

[18] *Quarterly Journal of Economics*, LXIII (1949), 476–506. In addition to his works already cited see especially his "Interregional and Regional Input-Output Analysis: A Model of Space-Economy," *The Review of Economics and Statistics*, XXXIII, No. 4 (1951), 318–328.

article was drawn upon freely for some of the data in the remaining part of this section.

The first attempt in this century to create a general location theory appeared in 1909 in the work of Alfred Weber.[19] Weber was interested in the historical sequence of locational patterns with special emphasis upon manufacturing industry. He conceived the optimum location for a given firm to be that position where aggregate cost was at a minimum in a *given* framework of areal patterns for the various locational factors (such as labor, market, raw materials, and power). But Weber did not create a general theory by which the spatial relationships of all economic activity can be expressed.

The following year both Bortkiewicz[20] and Schumpeter[21] wrote pleas for a general locational theory to augment partial locational theories such as Weber's. In 1913 Furlan[22] again raised the issue of the need for a general locational theory.

Weber's evolutionary approach was continued in the works of Englånder in the mid-1920's.[23] Another disciple of Weber was Ritschl.[24] At about the same time Predöhl[25]

[19] A. Weber, *Uber den standort der Industrien* (Tübingen, 1909). English translation: C. J. Friedrich, *Alfred Weber's Theory of the Location of Industry* (Chicago, 1929).

[20] F. Bortkiewicz, *Deutsche Literaturzeitung*, XXXI (1919).

[21] J. Schumpeter, *Jahrbuch für Gesetzgebung, Verwaltung, und Volkswirtschaft*, XXXIV, No. 3 (1910).

[22] V. Furlan, "Die Standorts probleme in der Volks-und Weltwirtschaftslehre," *Westwirtschaftliches Archiv*, II (1913), 1–34.

[23] O. Engländer, *Theorie des Güterverkehrs und der Frachtsätze* (Jena, 1924); and "Kritisches und Positives zu einer allgemeinen reinen Lehre vom Standort," *Zeitschrift fur Volkswirtschaft und Sozialpolitik*, V, Nos. 7–9 (1926).

[24] H. Ritschl, "Reine und historische Dynamik des Standortes der Erzeugungsweige," *Schmollers Jahrbuch*, LI (1927), 813–870.

[25] A. Predöhl, "Das Standortsproblem in der Wirtschaftstheorie," *Weltwirtschaftliches Archiv*, XXI (1925), 294–331; and "The Theory of Location in its Relation to General Economics," *Journal of Political Economy*, XXXVI (1928), 371–390.

made a plea for a spatial theory as an integral part of a general equilibrium theory of interdependent prices as developed by Walras, Pareto, or Cassel.

A few years later Palander, writing in Sweden, contributed the first major work outside of Germany in location theory.[26] He raised the question as to whether a solvable system of equations can be evolved for a space-economy. Concluding that it cannot, he abandoned the Walrasian system for a Weberian analysis stressing the need for recognizing the economic development process in understanding the locational patterns of activity.

In 1933 E. H. Chamberlin of Harvard University contributed a remarkable work, a pioneer work in monopolistic competition.[27] Although not treating of distance or spatial arrangement *per se*, it does admit of location as an important aspect of product differentiation.

During the time between the contributions of Predöhl and Palander, the German Weigmann published several important articles and books.[28] Isard points out that Weigmann has not been given proper acclaim. This is probably due to the vagueness and complexity of his style, which did not make for easy synthesis of his work with others. Weigmann conceived of space theory as a part of a general equilibrium theory and appreciated the necessity of introducing time relationships into locational analysis.

In recent years there has been a remarkable number of

[26] T. Palander, *Beitrage zur Standortstheorie* (Uppsala, 1935).

[27] E. H. C. Chamberlin, *The Theory of Monopolistic Competition* (Cambridge 1933).

[28] H. Weigmann, *Kritischer Beitrag zur Theorie des internationalen Handels* (Jena, 1926); "Ideen zu einer Theorie der Raumwirtschaft," *Weltwirtschaftliches Archiv*, XXXIV (1931), 1–40; "Standortstheorie und Raumwirtschaft," *Joh. Heinr. Von Thünen zum 150 Geburstag*, ed. by Seedorf and Jurgen (Rostock, 1933), 137–157; and *Politische Raumsordnung* (Hamburg, 1935).

contributions to space theory. Most important of these are the works of Lösch[29] and Hoover.[30] Lösch treats both aspects of space-economy theory, i.e., location of activity and spatial price equilibrium whereas Hoover's emphasis is only upon location and in a manner similar to Weber, i.e., a partial analysis rather than general theory.

It is not the intent of this study to collect, analyze, criticize, and summarize the contributions to space theory. Interested readers can find these tasks admirably performed in the papers by Isard previously referred to.

In addition to the contributions to theory in this century, there has been compiled an imposing mass of statistical findings concerning the relationship between distance and economic and social quantities. There has been concurrence in the conclusions concerning the attenuating influence of distance. This relationship has been called "the inverse distance relationship."

During the last century the work of Ravenstein concerning migration was probably the first (and possibly only) empirical test concerning the relationship between distance and certain social quantities. It will be recalled that Ravenstein discovered that a population center attracts migrants from and sends migrants to other centers in amounts that vary according to the sizes of the populations divided by the respective distances. More recently a great many similar findings have been made. Several typical examples are herein cited.

A number of studies have been made concerning residential propinquity of paired marriage license appli-

[29] A. Lösch, *Die raümliche Ordnung der Wirtschaft* (Jena, 1940). Happily this is now available in English translation as *The Economics of Location* (New Haven, 1954).

[30] E. M. Hoover, *The Location of Economic Activity* (New York, 1948).

cants.[31] In each case it was discovered that the number of paired applicants varied inversely with the distances between residences.

In 1940 Samuel Stouffer published a study[32] concerning change of family residence in Cleveland during 1933–1935. Once again there was an inverse relationship between the number of families moving and the distance they moved. Similar results were discovered by D. S. Thomas in research on interstate migration in the United States,[33] and by E. Isbell on internal migration in Sweden.[34]

The two men who probably have amassed the most impressive body of empirical data concerning the inverse distance relationship are Stewart of Princeton University and the late George K. Zipf of Harvard University.

Zipf's findings are summarized in his book, *Human Behavior and the Principle of Least Effort* (Cambridge: 1949).[35] An inverse distance relationship was found among the following: (1) the number of different news items in *The Chicago Tribune* (1937–1940) by other city datelines and the distance from Chicago; (2) number of obituary notices in *The New York Times* (1938–1941) by city and the distance from New York; (3) charge accounts of Jordan Marsh Company, Boston, in ninety-six cities and towns

[31] See J. H. S. Bossard, "Residential Propinquity as a Factor in Marriage Selection," *American Journal of Sociology*, XXXVIII (1932), 219–224; M. R. Davie and R. J. Reeves, "Propinquity of Residence before Marriage," *American Journal of Sociology*, XLIV (1939), 510–517; R. H. Abrams, "Residential Propinquity as a Factor in Marriage Selection," *American Sociological Review*, VIII (1943), 288–294.

[32] S. A. Stouffer, "Intervening Opportunities: A Theory Relating Mobility and Distance," *American Sociological Review* (1940), 845–867.

[33] D. S. Thomas, "Interstate Migration and Intervening Opportunities," *American Sociological Review*, VI (1941), 773–783.

[34] E. Isbell, "Internal Migration in Sweden and Intervening Opportunities," *American Sociological Review*, IX (1944), 627–639.

[35] See especially Chapter IX, "The Economy of Geography," 347–415.

in Maine, New Hampshire, and Massachusetts; (4) Railway Express movements by weight (May, 1939) between thirteen paired cities in the United States; (5) bus passengers (1933–1934) moving between twenty-nine paired United States cities; (6) railway passengers (1933) moving between wenty-nine paired United States cities; (7) airline passengers (1933) moving between twenty-nine paired United States cities; and (8) telephone messages between 311 paired cities in the United States (1940).

In each case allowance was made for the sizes of the cities so that the over-all relation was one that can be expressed as $P_1.P_2/d_{12}$ when P equals population and d equals distance. That is to say, there was a direct relationship with the product of the populations involved and an inverse one with the distance between these populations.

Stewart conceived of P/d as "Population Potential," previously referred to in this study and subsequently discussed. Although all the work of Stewart is not gathered together in one article, the best summary of his findings is in "The Development of Social Physics."[36]

The following are among the social quantities found by Stewart to be a function of potential of population: (1) attendance by state at certain "national" universities and at major fairs, etc., (2) long distance telephone calls, (3) interregional flow of bank checks and postal money orders, (4) miles of highway and railway per square mile in rural regions, and (5) farmland value per acre.

This list exhausts neither the observations nor the ideas of Stewart. Recourse is made later to certain other ideas of Stewart.

This, then, concludes a brief historical survey of man's considerations of the dimensions of society with special

[36] *American Journal of Physics*, XVIII, No. 5 (1950), 239–253.

reference to economic activity. These dimensions have been considered to be mass, time, and space. If disproportionate emphasis has been given to the empirical studies of spatial relationships, it has been done purposely. One of the objectives of the major part of this study is to investigate the geographical (i.e., spatial) distribution of farm prices of certain agricultural commodities. An attempt will be made to do this in terms of a dimensional analysis, using concepts and measures especially developed to express time, space, and quantity or mass relationships. These are the aspects that all economic phenomena have in common and that should be included in an analysis because of their persisting and general nature, as contrasted with certain particular and accidental influences that also affect price.

2

Geography and Economics

As has been indicated, an attempt will be made to analyze the geographical variation of farm prices of certain agricultural commodities in terms of basic physical dimensions such as time, distance, and mass or size of given populations, whether or not those populations be comprised of human beings, bushels of wheat, or pounds of shorn wool.

A. Demand and Population Potential

From these fundamental physical factors secondary quantities can be derived which can be very useful in the analysis of economic activities. One of these is "Population Potential."

For the purposes of social science it may be useful to assume that any concentration of population exerts an influence varying directly with the size of the population. It is logical to assume that this influence is diminished by distance. This influence exists throughout the area occupied by the population and beyond this area, losing in intensity as distance increases. There exists, then, a field of force around a given population cluster and at any point in the field the intensity can be calculated by dividing the size of the population by the distance involved. Such a field has been called a "demographic field"[1] by Stewart of Princeton University.

The level of the intensity at any point in the demographic field can be called the population potential at

[1] John Q. Stewart, "Demographic Gravitation: Evidence and Applications," *Sociometry*, XI (1948), 31–58.

that point. Therefore, if city *A* is 900 miles from city *B*, then the potential in city *B* created by, say, 450,000 people in city *A* is 500 persons per mile. As one approached city *A* the calculated potential would be higher because of the decreasing distance. Of course, the reverse would obtain for more distant points.

The total population potential at any one point in the United States could be computed approximately by dividing the country into a number of areas, and then dividing the population of each area by its average distance to the point under consideration. The resultant quotients could be summed to give the total population potential at that point, potential being expressed in terms of the number of persons per mile or some other convenient unit of population per unit of linear measurement.

This process could be repeated for a great number of points. Lines connecting points of equal value could be drawn on a map on which the spot values of population potential had been plotted. These "equipotential" lines would be analogous to the contour lines of the topographic map. They could be plotted in precisely the same way, considering the spot potential values as spot elevations. By use of this isogram technique, an estimation of population potential may be made for any point in the United States.

The population potential at a point also can be regarded as a measure of the aggregate proximity of people to that point. Every person makes a contribution, which is smaller the farther away he is.

In so calculating population potentials, each person is considered to be of unitary weight. However, it would seem logical to weight people by their incomes if application of population is to be made in the analysis of economic phenomena. Each person is not an equally effective economic unit. A potential of population so calculated as to consider not only numbers of people and their locations but also their incomes might well be called Gross Economic Population Potential.

Figure 2 (in Chapter 3) is a map of Gross Economic Population Potential in the United States (1940–49 average). In computing the data for this map the geographic center of each state was used as a control point.[a] Then measurements were made of the distances from each control point in turn to all others. For the purposes of this study these distances were measured in terms of one-hundred-mile units and were rounded off to the nearest half. Table VIII (see Chapter 3) is the table of distance factors so measured and used in the calculation of the various space potentials in this study.

For the human populations, census data and intercensal estimates were used for each year in the ten-year period 1940–49. An arithmetic mean was calculated for the population of each state and this figure was used as the average population in effect in each state for this period.

As has been suggested, each state's human population was weighted by its average annual per capita income for the same period.

Here a simple arithmetic mean of the annual income payments to individuals would not suffice as a weighting factor since populations of all the states changed from year to year. So, a weighted arithmetic mean of income was constructed for each state and this weighted average was used.

If total income payments to individuals can be identi-

[a] Sources for these data and all other data as well as notes on the construction of all tables and figures in this study are contained in the special appendix at the end.

fied with total effective demand in a society (i.e., total possible claims that can be made on economic goods), then a Gross Economic Population Potential map can be looked upon as a map showing the geographic distribution of effective demand.

Spatial dimensions have thereby been added to the aggregate of income. It is submitted that national income (a concept well known and frequently used by the Economist) portrayed in this manner is an improvement over just a single national aggregate total in that it is a closer approximation of the reality of income since it recognizes the fact of its spatial dimensions.

The numerical values of Gross Economic Population Potential can also serve as measures of market accessibility. That is to say, aggregate purchasing power or market demand has been given its spatial distribution and the way in which the proximity to the total market varies geographically in the United States can be observed. The map indicates the areal variation in the intensity of demand.

In the United States, demand, so defined, is most intense in the Middle Atlantic States. The level of high intensity continues into southern New England like a plateau, but it is a steep-sided plateau and the intensity of demand and proximity to market drop off rapidly in up-country New England.

A ridge of high potential extends through the Middle West, dropping off gradually to the westward. Actually, the potential drops off by decreasing amounts, a fact which can be determined by observing the increasing distance between equipotential lines (with a constant interval), as one proceeds from Illinois to the very low values of the Intermontane Basin states. Note also, the low values in the Southeastern states.

A very interesting fact can also be found in the circumstances of the Pacific Coast states, primarily California. Here large local populations with their high incomes have helped to produce a higher level of intensity than in the vast Intermontane area to the east of California. In many ways California is indeed an economic island.

Very significantly, then, there is a "highland" of demand centered in the Middle Atlantic states trending downward in all directions from this plateau, though not at the same slope in each direction. There is also a small, yet distinct and separate, locally elevated "highland" in California.

This map (Figure 2) has been called a map of *Gross* Economic Population Potential. It is "gross" in that it represents the over-all areal pattern of effective demand.

The spatial pattern of demand for any one product could be considered as being derived from this areal distribution of Gross Economic Population Potential. For a given commodity, custom, income elasticity of demand, and prices of substitutes would be among the other important factors modifying the economic effect of a population and its income in a given area.

For the purposes of this study, the geographical distribution of Gross Economic Population Potential is accepted as the areal pattern of variation in the intensity of demand for each commodity analyzed. In the subsequent multiple correlation analyses of the geographic variations of farm prices of certain agricultural commodities, the same independent variable representing the demand force influencing prices is used for each commodity. This variable is the Gross Economic Population Potential calculated for each of the forty-eight state-centered control points. It was from these data that Figure 2, the map of Gross Economic Population Potential, was constructed.

A choice had to be made between developing a map of areally distributed intensity of demand for a given commodity (recognizing such things as income elasticity, prices of substitutes, custom or tastes, and the like) or a single map of over-all effective demand which would serve as the demand factor in the analysis of the geographic variation of prices of several commodities. The latter alternative was chosen, inasmuch as it was felt that the purpose of this study was not to examine *all* possible factors influencing prices, but rather to develop the theory of space potential and demonstrate its usefulness as a type of methodology in Economic Geography.

Existing topics in demand theory are not being investigated. It is rather the purpose, in part, of this study to augment the existing notions about demand by adding the very real aspect of areal distribution and geographical variation in its intensity in a space continuum. Then, too, the level of income elasticity of demand, tastes, etc., are peculiar or unique for each commodity, whereas all commodities share in common the fact that the demand for them is areally distributed (however different their individual geographies might be) and that they all exist in a space continuum.

Space is a continuum and all distances and directions in the area in which an economic system functions are interdependent. A theory of Economics which includes the concept of the interdependent nature and the simultaneous determination of all prices should also include a recognition of this interdependence of all distances and directions. It is submitted that the 2,304 individual distance measurements used in the construction of the map of Gross Economic Potential sufficiently approximate this ideal circumstance with regard to the demand influence in price.

It must be recognized that the intensity of demand varies through time as well as through space. The patterns of the temporal variations of the intensity of demand for various commodities would, of course, differ. If a separate map of demand were to be used for each commodity then another variable representing demand time potentials might be considered in the correlation analysis of farm prices.

However, because of the lack of detailed data that could be readily used concerning the temporal variation in demand and since the decision has been made to use one basic set of values for the demand factor, time variations in demand for individual commodities have not been included (although admittedly they exist) in the analyses in this study. This topic is discussed further in Chapter 4.

B. Supply, and Product-space and Product-time Potentials

If the interdependence of all distances and directions in the space continuum of a society be an important consideration in demand, so, it might be argued, must it be recognized in an analysis of the supply of a given commodity.

Just as a map of potential of human population indicates the geographical distribution of proximity to people, so would a similar map using a nonhuman population such as wheat show the geographical distribution of proximity to that wheat. Therefore, areal variations in the intensity of the wheat space potential similarly indicate variations in the accessibility of places to the aggregate wheat productions. Where the space potential of the commodity is highest, there is the point which has the greatest proximity or accessibility to the commodity. There the supply force influencing price is considered to be most intense.

As one moved out to points of lower and lower space potential, he would be moving to points which are successively less accessible to the commodity spacewise and at which the effective supply factor influencing price becomes less and less intense.

Figures 3, 4, 5, and 6 (see Chapter 3) all are maps of Product Supply Space Potential constructed from values computed in the same manner as Population Potential.

Once again for each commodity state centers were used as control points. The same 2,304 individual distance measurements were used to approximate all the possible distances in the space continuum.

The resulting "contour" maps of Supply Space Potential for the commodities do differ significantly because of the considerable differences in the actual geographical distribution of production of these commodities. Commodity "population" totals vary greatly from state to state for a given commodity and also in a given state from commodity to commodity. This results in substantially different patterns of "contours" on the several Product Supply Space Potential maps. Individual maps in the Product Supply Space Potential Series are utilized in a later section of this study.

Not only are all units of a commodity not homogeneous because they may be produced at different places, but they also are nonhomogeneous if they are produced at different instants in a time continuum of interdependent time intervals. Prices will reflect current production, past production (because of storage possibilities), *and* customary or anticipated future production.

A concentrated output of a commodity exerts an influence on price extending through the period of time of its production (a day, a week, or however arbitrarily defined) and, beyond this period, losing in force as the time becomes longer and longer. There is, then, a peak of intensity at the instant of production of a given amount of a commodity and for any point in time removed from the period of production the intensity can be calculated by dividing the size of the output by the number of time units involved. Such a value might well be called "Product Supply Time Potential" and could be expressed in terms of production units per time unit, as for example, bushels per month.

It may have occurred to the reader that in the calculation of the various space potentials in this study only the shorter arc of the great circle on the earth's surface between two places was used for the distance factor. On a sphere with a circumference of about 25,000 miles the greater arc can be ignored as of no significance in calculations of potential as long as the area under consideration has a maximum dimension considerably less than half this amount. Such is the case in the United States with 2,700 miles the largest value, this being the distance between the center of California and the center of Maine. The situation would be somewhat different if one had to make decisions about places halfway around the world from each other.[3]

With time potentials, a somewhat similar problem *cannot* be ignored. If the "average annual" farm price to be analyzed in a certain place is really the price for a commodity produced only in August, can one justifiably assume that all time influences affecting that average price are contained only within that calendar year? If such a situation be so, then the time difference between March and November is eight months.

But if one recognizes that annual averages are just an

[3] Dr. John Q. Stewart has tentatively suggested, in conversation with the author, that the chords be used.

arbitrarily convenient way of stating prices, then one must be prepared to recognize that a time difference of only four months exists between the March of one year and the November of the preceding year. It then seems logical that both time differences should be included in a series of time differences representing all possible time relationships in a time continuum.

It might be argued that more than two differences should be recognized between any two months. In the case of March and November, for a given March not only is it separated from November by 4 and 8 months, but also 16 and 20, 28 and 32, 36 and 40, etc., as one considers past and subsequent years.

However, experimentation with the data shows that whereas the curves on the charts of time potential (the construction of which are explained subsequently) do differ in appearance, depending upon whether just one or both time differences are used, the inclusion of more and more pairs of time differences serves only to increase the values for all months on the charts by smaller and smaller amounts without changing their relative position, while also adding substantially to the labor of calculation.

Accordingly, 156 individual time differences were used to approximate the time continuum, the time unit being the month. See Table IX for this information. Data were obtained from several sources concerning the harvest times for the various commodities. An average time was estimated for the production of a commodity in a given state.[4] Then, totals of production for each month were compiled (see Table III). The total for each month was considered to be concentrated at mid-month.

[4] Note that in the case of two widely separated seasons of production in a state, e.g., early spring and late autumn, two separate time potentials (but just one space potential) are computed and linked in the subsequent correlation analysis with their corresponding prices.

The total time potential for the middle of any month was computed approximately by dividing the production of each other month by the two appropriate time differences and summing the quotients to give the total product time potential for that point in time expressed in terms of units of production per month.

This process could be repeated for each of the twelve months and the values plotted on a graph with the appropriate curve drawn to show the variation throughout the year of the product time potential. The Product Supply Time Potential at any harvest date can be readily estimated from the data so compiled. See especially Figures 7, 8, 9, and 10 for the various Product Supply Time Potential graphs.

The time potential at a given instant of time can be regarded as a measure of the nearness or proximity in time of all production of the product to that instant of time. Every unit of the product makes a contribution to the total time potential, which is less the farther removed the unit is in time of production (either past or future) from the instant of time concerned.

Of course, such a calculation of time potential assumes a symmetry between the effect of past and future time differences. Further study might reveal that this symmetry is not so, but for lack of data this simplifying assumption of symmetry is made. Even so, this assumption of symmetry is not without precedent. In the calculation of "present value" of either a past investment or a future acquisition, discount rate or interest rate is applied symmetrically.[5]

[5] J. H. Moore, *Handbook of Financial Mathematics* (New York, 1940). See especially Chapter II, "Present Value and Simple Discount," 29–60.

C. The Geography of Price

"The geography of price" shall be understood to mean (for the purposes of this study) the areal or spatial distribution of farm prices of various agricultural commodities in the United States. The prices to be "explained" are the average prices by states for the ten-year period 1940–49 for the various agricultural commodities considered, which include wheat, potatoes, onions, and strawberries. They represent the prices paid to farmers (at the farm) and are considered as the dependent variable in the multiple linear correlations analyses in Chapter 3.

The task, then, is to account for the variation from place to place in these prices. The explanation of the overall level of prices is a problem in Economics, but the explanation of spatial variation in these prices is a problem for the Economic Geographer.

A valid economic generalization—the Law of Supply and Demand—contends that price is a function of supply and demand. Price varies directly with demand and inversely with supply.

It is here contended that any geographic variation in the intensity of these factors would, therefore, tend to produce geographic variation in the price of the commodity, the hypothesis then being that price tends to vary directly with Demand Space Potential and inversely with both Supply Space Potential and Supply Time Potential.

Price at a point in space is a function of these three independent variables and geographical variation in the level of this price results from the concomitant geographical variation in the intensities of these factors.

Herein lies the essence of the Economic Geographer's contribution to the analysis of economic phenomena. His concern lies in the areal differentiation of economic phenomena and his objectives are to describe geographical patterns and to discover the causes (and consequences) of these given areal distributions.

Chapter 3 of this study deals with several tests of the hypothesis just suggested. Stated formally as a hypothesis in Economic Geography it might be as follows: "Price varies from place to place directly with Demand Space Potential[a] and inversely with Supply Space Potential and Supply Time Potential."

If these relationships actually exist, then the regression coefficient in a multiple linear correlation analysis of price and demand potential should have a positive sign and the other two regression coefficients (i.e., the regression of price on Supply Space Potential and on Supply Time Potential) should have negative signs. The size of the regression coefficients depends in part upon the units in which the variables are stated but is of importance because it furnishes a basis for the calculation of the relative importance of the individual variables, which can be expected to be different for different commodities. The adequacy of the estimating equations developed for predicting price at a place will also be shown by a measure called the *Standard Error of Estimate.* And the over-all correlation, or the amount of the variation "explained" by the formula used, also will be indicated by the *Coefficient of Multiple Correlation.* These terms are explained in detail in Chapter 3.

[a] The concept of Demand Space Potential is called Gross Economic Population in this study.

3

Testing the Hypothesis and the Commodity Analyses

A. Methodology

In the previous chapter, it was suggested that the variation from place to place in the farm price of an agricultural commodity was the result of variation from place to place in the intensity of the demand for and the supply of that commodity. In addition, it was submitted that the variation in the time of production from place to place also influenced farm price.

The following concepts were developed to represent the above factors: Gross Economic Population Potential, Product Supply Space Potential, and Product Supply Time Potential.

It was also reasoned that there is a direct relationship between price and Gross Economic Population Potential and an inverse relationship between price and both Product Supply Space Potential and Product Supply Time Potential. These relationships were stated as the hypothesis of this study.

In keeping with customary procedure and for the sake of convenience each of the variables is given a concise notation. Hereinafter farm price will be considered as the dependent variable and the three other factors as the independent variables.

The following symbols are used:

X_1, Commodity Farm Price per unit
X_2, Gross Economic Population Potential
X_3, Product Supply Space Potential
X_4, Product Supply Time Potential

If it is further assumed that there is a functional relationship between the dependent variable and each of the independent variables and that these relationships are of a quantitative nature, then an appropriate tool for analyzing and measuring the relationships and stating them in a simple formula is statistical correlation.

Stated in a general way, regardless of the commodity or the units in which it is to be analyzed, the estimating equation used to test the hypothesis in this paper is:

$$Xc_{1.234} = a_{1.234} + b_{12.34}X_2 + b_{13.24}X_3 + b_{14.23}X_4$$

The dependent variable farm price is labeled $Xc_{1.234}$ since it is an estimate of X_1 derived from the variables X_2, X_3, and X_4. The formula stated above is a multiple linear regression equation. Least squares correlation methods were used.

Finding the proper values for the estimating equation for each commodity requires the simultaneous solution (for each commodity) of the four normal equations:

$$\Sigma X_1 = Na_{1.234} + b_{12.34}\,\Sigma X_2 + b_{13.24}\,\Sigma X_3 + b_{14.23}\,\Sigma X_4$$

$$\Sigma X_1X_2 = a_{1.234}\,\Sigma X_2 + b_{12.34}\,\Sigma X_2^2 + b_{13.24}\,\Sigma X_2X_3 + b_{14.23}\,\Sigma X_2X_4$$

$$\Sigma X_1X_3 = a_{1.234}\,\Sigma X_3 + b_{12.34}\,\Sigma X_2X_3 + b_{13.24}\,\Sigma X_3^2 + b_{14.23}\,\Sigma X_3X_4$$

$$\Sigma X_1X_4 = a_{1.234}\,\Sigma X_4 + b_{12.34}\,\Sigma X_2X_4 + b_{13.24}\,\Sigma X_3X_4 + b_{14.23}\,\Sigma X_4^2$$

Some expedition can be gained by restating each equation in terms of the deviations from the means of the above extensions. This results in the first equation becoming zero and leaving then three to be solved. In the solving of the equations for this study, this latter method was employed and an internal *S* check was included to insure the accuracy of the arithmetic involved.

Before going further, it is perhaps desirable to discuss the meanings of the four constants in the multiple linear regression equation used in this study.

The constant $a_{1\cdot 234}$ is the hypothetical value for X_1 (i.e., farm price) when the independent variables have a value of zero, or if there were (in terms of this study) no geographical variation in the intensities of the three independent variables.

The b constants, variously called the *net regression coefficients* or the *net coefficients of estimation,* indicate the change in X_1 associated with the change in an accompanying independent variable when allowance has been made for the other independent variables.

Hence, $b_{12\cdot 34}$ is an estimate of the number of units change in X_1 (farm price) for each one unit change in X_2 (Gross Economic Population Potential) independent of the variations in X_3 (Product Supply Space Potential) and X_4 (Product Supply Time Potential). Similarly $b_{13.24}$ is an estimate of the net effect, in terms of the units unused, of Product Supply Space Potential on price, and $b_{14.23}$ estimates the regression of price on Product Supply Time Potential with the effect of the other two independent variables removed.

Although the various regression coefficients are called "net," they are so, only with regard to the other variables considered. They do remain "gross" however with regard to all the possible factors not considered in the correlation.

The estimate of farm price for any place, then, is the sum of the net amounts associated with each independent variable plus the value for $a_{1.234}$.

Obviously, the actual size of the net regression coefficient depends in part upon the units in which the variables are stated. But when taken with certain other values these net regression coefficients make possible the calculation of measures estimating the relative importance of each independent variable. More of this later.

Despite the fact that the actual size of the net regression coefficients depends partly upon the units in which the variables are stated, this circumstance does not affect the nature of the relationship between the dependent variable and each of the independent ones as to whether it be direct or inverse. It was hypothesized that the farm price varied directly with Gross Economic Population Potential and inversely with both Product Space Supply Potential and Product Time Supply Potential. If this be the actual circumstance, then the sign of $b_{12 \cdot 34}$ should be positive and the signs of both $b_{13 \cdot 24}$ and $b_{14 \cdot 23}$ should be negative. Here, then, is an important check on the validity of the hypothesis. In the analysis of each individual commodity particular attention will be paid to the signs of the various net regression coefficients.

In addition to these measures that describe the functional relationships between the variables, other measures of importance should be considered.

These include one which indicates the variation of the actual values of the dependent variable from its estimated values. This concept, identified as $S_{1.234}$ and known as the *standard error of estimate*, measures the amount of variation left in the dependent variable which has not been "explained" by the estimating equation. It is stated in the same units as the dependent variable and hence gives in absolute terms an indication of the dependability of the estimates. The interpretation of standard errors of estimate is analogous to that of standard deviations for arithmetic means. The estimated values plus and minus one $S_{1.234}$ establish a range within which two thirds (actually 68.27 per cent) of the prices lie.

Another important measure is one showing the degree of relationship or correlation between the dependent variable and the independent ones regardless of the units in which the variables are expressed. This *coefficient of multiple correlation* is identified as $R_{1.234}$ and ranges in value from zero to one, that is from no correlation whatsoever to perfect correlation. Unlike the analogous measure for simple linear correlation, R has no sign since the association may be negative with some variables and positive with others.

If more and more pertinent factors could be introduced into the analysis, R would approach that of perfect correlation. If all factors influencing the value of the dependent variable could be included, R would be one.

It should be noted that the purpose of this study is not to discover and utilize all the factors necessary to yield perfect correlation, but rather to develop a dimensional analysis of economic activity using the primary physical concepts of mass, time, and space, which factors are included in the basis reality of all phenomena. It is to be hoped that the concepts developed will help to furnish another step toward the ultimate development in economic theory of a General Equilibrium Price Theory recognizing the dimensions of space and time.

As suggested before, the absolute values of the b coefficients are influenced by the units in which the variables are stated. However, by utilizing these data, estimates of the relative importance of each independent variable can be made.

Two separate measures of the *relative* "net" importance of each independent variable can be readily computed. These are (1) the *beta coefficients* or $\beta_{12.34}$, $\beta_{13.24}$, and $\beta_{14.23}$ and (2) the *coefficients of separate determination* or $d^2 12.34$, $d^2 13.24$, and $d^2 14.23$. The beta coefficients are calculated by stating each of the variables in units of its own individual standard deviation. Hence:

$$\beta_{12.34} = b_{12.34} \frac{\sigma_2}{\sigma_1};$$

$$\beta_{13.24} = b_{13.24} \frac{\sigma_3}{\sigma_1};$$

$$\beta_{14.23} = b_{14.23} \frac{\sigma_4}{\sigma_1}.$$

The coefficients of separate determination split up the value of $R^2_{1.234}$ into three components. (Note that $R^2_{1.234}$ or the squared coefficient of multiple linear correlation is called the coefficient of determination.) Hence:

$$d^2_{12.34} = \frac{b_{12.34}\ \Sigma x_1 x_2}{\Sigma x_1^2};$$

$$d^2_{13.24} = \frac{b_{13.24}\ \Sigma x_1 x_3}{\Sigma x_1^2};$$

$$d^2_{14.23} = \frac{b_{14.23}\ \Sigma x_1 x_4}{\Sigma x_1^2}.$$

The sum of these three coefficients equals the value of $R^2_{1.234}$. From the individual d^2 a "d" (coefficient of separate correlation) might be computed, but since d^2 can be negative, d cannot always be computed directly.

It must be remembered also that although the signs of the net regression coefficients (i.e., $b_{12.34}$, $b_{13.24}$, and $b_{14.23}$) indicate whether the relationships be direct of inverse, this is not necessarily the case with the coefficients of separate determination. It *is* the case with the beta coefficients, however.

The individual $R_{1.234}$ values computed from the data available measure the correlation in that data. Since the commodity data are, in a sense, samples from the entire statistical universes, an allowance should be made for this circumstance and recognition of the fact that correlation values thus obtained may overestimate the true population values especially if the sample is small. The best estimate of correlation in the population is calculated from the formula:

$$\bar{R}_{1.234} = \sqrt{\frac{R^2_{1.234}(N-1)-(m-1)}{N-m}}$$

where N is the sample size and m is the number of degrees of freedom lost in computing $R_{1.234}$ (i.e., the number of constants in the estimating equation).

Table XIX gives the values for each commodity analyzed for each of the measures discussed above.

In addition, Table XX includes a test of the significance of the value of $\bar{R}_{1.234}$. The level of significance used is one chance in twenty (i.e., the assumed fiducial limit is 5 per cent).

There is then less than one chance in twenty that a value as high as the one given for each commodity in Table XX can arise owing to sampling variation. If the computed $\bar{R}_{1.234}$ exceeds this figure, then the multiple association may be considered to be significant.

B. Commodity Analyses

To test the hypothesis that the geographical variation in the farm price of an agricultural commodity is associated with the concomitant geographical variation in Gross Economic Population Potential, Product Supply Space Potential, and Product Supply Time Potential, certain basic raw data are required to construct these variables. These data include population, per capita income, farm price per unit, and total units produced for each of several commodities and harvest dates.

So as to lessen the probability of using abnormal

values, averages for the ten year period 1940–49 were used. Table I includes the average annual production and the average farm price for wheat, potatoes, onions, and strawberries for the United States for this time period.

These United States aggregates for the four commodities were subject to the dimensional analysis outlined in Chapter II.

Table I

UNITED STATES—AVERAGE ANNUAL PRODUCTION AND AVERAGE FARM PRICE FOR WHEAT, POTATOES, ONIONS, AND STRAWBERRIES (1940–49)

A *Commodity*	B *Production*	C *Farm Price*
Wheat	1,071,347,000 bushels	$1.51 per bushel
Potatoes	410,475,000 bushels	$1.22 per bushel
Onions	37,892,000 sacks (50 lbs. each)	$1.31 per sack
Strawberries	8,964,000 crates (24 quarts each)	$6.36 per crate

SOURCES: See Appendix.

The data of human population and income used in this study are summarized in the following table.

Table II

UNITED STATES—AVERAGE POPULATION, AVERAGE ANNUAL PER CAPITA INCOME, AND AVERAGE ECONOMIC POPULATION (1940–49)

A *Population*	B *Per Capita Income*	C *Economic Population* ($A \times B$)
137,535,000	$1,075	$147,726,000,000

SOURCES: See Appendix.

However, annual totals or averages for the United States as a whole obscure any temporal relationships within the year and any spatial relationships within the country.

Were, for example, the 410,475,000 bushels of potatoes which the United States, on the average, produced each year in the period 1940–49 all produced at one place and at one time or was production spread over many areas in the United States and through considerable time within the year?

Table III shows that there were considerable differences among the months in the production of the commodities for which the annual totals are given in Table I. Monthly production totals were compiled using harvest date and production data by states. These harvest dates are included in the tables of production, price, and harvest date(s) of the individual commodities by state. (See Tables XI, XII, XIII, and XIV.)

Table III

MONTHLY PRODUCTION IN UNITED STATES (1940–49 AVERAGE) OF WHEAT, POTATOES, ONIONS, AND STRAWBERRIES

Month	*Commodity*			
	Wheat 1,000 *bushels*	*Potatoes* 1,000 *bushels*	*Onions* 1,000 *sacks* (50 *lbs. each*)	*Strawberries* 1,000 *crates* (24 *quarts each*)
January	0	0	0	0
February	0	0	0	358
March	0	4,306	0	0
April	0	4,648	3,907	1,393
May	0	8,989	2,926	2,313
June	193,509	38,633	266	4,900
July	507,485	22,808	8,346	0
August	370,353	25,224	9,507	0
September	0	112,757	12,940	0
October	0	193,110	0	0
November	0	0	0	0
December	0	0	0	0
Totals	1,071,347	410,475	37,892	8,964

SOURCES: See Appendix.

Not only was the aggregate production of any commodity spread unevenly through time intervals, but also distributed over many areas in a very uneven fashion.

Complete knowledge of the spatial distribution of production would require that the exact location, for example, of the production of every grain of wheat be known; but such exactness cannot be realized. A knowledge of location of production by counties would be perhaps an adequate compromise. But even that is too "fine-grained" for the purpose of this study. Instead, the manner in which the other data were available and computational difficulties, suggested that states be used as the geographical units of association.

Table V gives the production by states for the average annual wheat, potato, onion, and strawberry crops during the ten-year period 1940–49.

For the sake of convenience and brevity in this and other tables each state was given a number and the same numerical designation applies to a given state throughout the study.

Table IV gives the numerical designation for each state and Figure I gives its location. Figure I also indicates the geographical center of each state. These data are utilized subsequently.

Table IV

NUMERICAL DESIGNATION FOR EACH STATE IN THE UNITED STATES

1. Washington	*13.* South Dakota	*25.* Mississippi	*37.* Virginia
2. Oregon	*14.* Nebraska	*26.* Alabama	*38.* Maryland and Dist. of Col.
3. California	*15.* Kansas	*27.* Tennessee	*39.* Delaware
4. Nevada	*16.* Oklahoma	*28.* Kentucky	*40.* New Jersey
5. Idaho	*17.* Texas	*29.* Indiana	*41.* Pennsylvania
6. Utah	*18.* Louisiana	*30.* Michigan	*42.* New York
7. Arizona	*19.* Arkansas	*31.* Ohio	*43.* Connecticut
8. New Mexico	*20.* Missouri	*32.* West Virginia	*44.* Rhode Island
9. Colorado	*21.* Iowa	*33.* Georgia	*45.* Massachusetts
10. Wyoming	*22.* Minnesota	*34.* Florida	*46.* Vermont
11. Montana	*23.* Wisconsin	*35.* South Carolina	*47.* New Hampshire
12. North Dakota	*24.* Illinois	*36.* North Carolina	*48.* Maine

SOURCES: See Appendix.

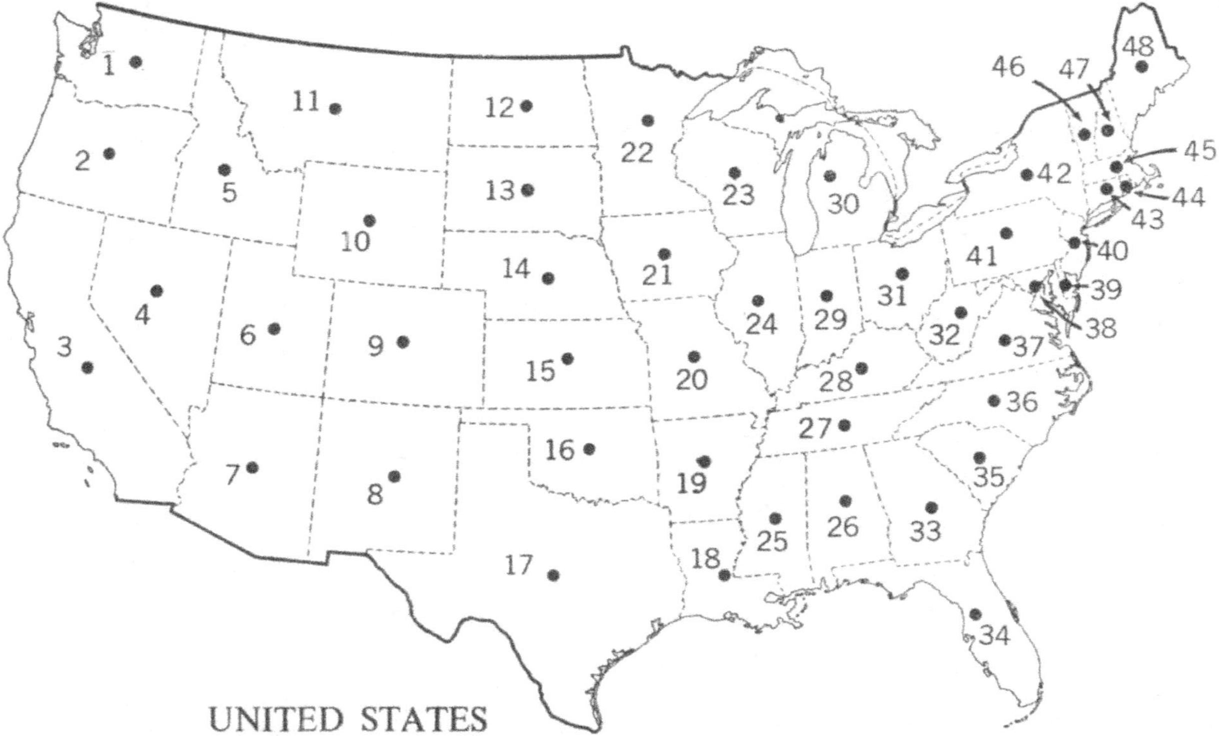

UNITED STATES
GEOGRAPHIC CENTERS

Geographic center and reference number for each state in the United States *Sources: see appendix*

Table V

UNITED STATES—AVERAGE ANNUAL PRODUCTION OF WHEAT, POTATOES, ONIONS, AND STRAWBERRIES BY STATES (1940–49)

A State	*B* Wheat	*C* Potatoes	*D* Onions	*E* Strawberries	*A* State	*B* Wheat	*C* Potatoes	*D* Onions	*E* Strawberries
1	61,580	9,524	849	614	33	2,470	1,517	167	1
2	22,666	10,736	2,565	949	34	—	4,306	—	258
3	10,969	34,039	4,533	638	35	3,135	2,457	24	—
4	529	524	217	—	36	6,801	9,295	314	—
5	31,154	37,379	2,078	—	37	8,117	8,998	333	79
6	6,937	2,801	646	57	38	6,840	1,906	228	—
7	575	1,179	339	—	39	1,231	342	84	—
8	4,176	283	266	—	40	1,440	11,213	188	664
9	35,996	17,313	5,186	—	41	18,440	19,176	168	98
10	4,976	2,219	—	—	42	8,367	32,145	312	6,593
11	68,845	2,100	—	—	43	4	3,440	—	—
12	137,943	19,589	—	—	44	2	1,263	—	—
13	41,358	2,435	—	—	45	6	3,214	—	575
14	63,652	10,542	—	—	46	3	1,430	—	—
15	193,512	1,824	87	65	47	1	1,102	—	—
16	73,998	1,540	98	72	48	26	59,654	—	—
17	63,486	4,648	5,898	56	Total	1,071,347	410,475	37,892	8,964
18	18	2,346	161	931					
19	389	3,100	—	748					
20	22,658	3,446	—	236					
21	4,387	3,232	332	54					
22	22,004	18,147	1,563	—					
23	1,912	12,708	744	168					
24	28,897	1,981	719	182					
25	278	1,632	—	7					
26	200	4,186	—	183					
27	4,762	3,088	—	586					
28	5,401	3,546	19	316					
29	29,529	4,502	882	153					
30	23,553	17,755	3,459	703					
31	46,592	7,731	265	234					

A. State—see Table IV and Figure 1.
B. Wheat—thousands of bushels.
C. Potatoes—thousands of bushels.
D. Onions—thousands of sacks (50 lbs. each).
E. Strawberries—thousands of sacks (24 quarts each).

SOURCES: See Appendix.

UNITED STATES—AVERAGE FARM PRICES PAID FOR WHEAT, POTATOES, ONIONS, AND STRAWBERRIES (1940–49) BY STATES

A State	*B* Wheat	*C* Potatoes	*D* Onions	*E* Strawberries	*A* State	*B* Wheat	*C* Potatoes	*D* Onions	*E* Strawberries
1	144	128	10,093	560	33	163	152	161	—
2	147	136	106	542	34	—	181	—	924
3	161	128,143	150,125,119	864,772	35	168	150	—	687
4	149	144	125	—	36	171	127	—	664
5	139	94	74	—	37	166	133	165	570
6	141	127	117	884	38	163	138	—	615
7	165	158	192,106	—	39	165	148	—	608
8	144	—	169	—	40	163	121	155	670
9	145	121	102	—	41	161	144	160	718
10	142	130	—	—	42	162	130	152	739
11	145	138	—	—	43	—	—	—	—
12	155	103	—	—	44	—	—	—	—
13	152	138	—	—	45	—	—	123	—
14	150	110	—	—	46	—	—	—	—
15	150	115	132	561	47	—	—	—	—
16	147	133	108	539	48	—	109	—	—
17	146	160	174,164	741	Weighted				
18	—	140	181	780	average	151	122	131	696
19	151	134	—	541					
20	154	126	—	645					
21	152	—	135,116	668					
22	157	111	125	—					
23	152	126	133	626					
24	156	—	131	602					
25	155	143	—	—					
26	164	129	—	520					
27	166	135	—	522					
28	161	138	140	610					
29	159	—	139	662					
30	161	126	142	632					
31	159	—	163	696					
32	164	—	—	—					

A. State—See Table IV and Figure 1.
B. Wheat farm price in cents per bushel.
C. Potato farm price in cents per bushel.
D. Onion farm price in cents per sack (50 lbs. each).
E. Strawberry farm price in cents per crate (24 quarts each).

SOURCES: See Appendix.

Table VI shows the considerable geographical variation in the farm prices for the same commodities during the same ten-year period.

Similarly, the population and the annual income of the United States were neither gathered together in one place nor evenly distributed over the nearly three million square miles of the country during the ten-year period 1940–49.

Consequently, Table VII was included to show the uneven geographical distribution of population and per capita income. A column entitled Economic Population (the product of population times per capita income), which is equal to total income payments to individuals, was included because this has been considered in this study to represent the economically effective population.

To convert both the income-weighted population and the commodity production data into Space Potentials (i.e., Gross Economic Population Potential and Product Supply Space Potential as described in Chapter II) the distances between all control points (i.e., the geographic centers of the assumed areas) and each one in turn were required. For this study total production and population data were broken down into state values. Then, so that one table of distances could be used for computing all Space Potentials, the production for a state was assumed to be concentrated at the geographic center of that state. These centers then represent 48 control points. Table VIII contains the 2,304 individual distances between the 48 state-centered control points, these distances standing for all the interrelated distances in the space continuum known as the United States. The values of potential calculated for each geographic control point are the data from which a map of potentials could be drawn using logical contouring.

BASIC POPULATION AND INCOME DATA FOR UNITED STATES (1940–49 AVERAGES) BY STATES

A State	*B* Population in Thousands	*C* Annual per Capita Income in Dollars	*D* Economic Population in Millions of Dollars	*A* State	*B* Population in Thousands	*C* Annual per Capita Income in Dollars	*D* Economic Population in Millions of Dollars
1	2,125	1,282	2,724	31	7,259	1,205	8,746
2	1,303	1,161	1,513	32	1,843	782	1,441
3	9,042	1,413	12,777	33	3,236	687	2,223
4	142	1,460	208	34	2,362	904	2,135
5	525	991	520	35	1,944	615	1,195
6	620	981	608	36	3,668	681	2,498
7	636	906	576	37	3,082	867	2,672
8	557	782	435	38	2,979	1,271	3,787
9	1,168	1,062	1,241	39	291	1,365	397
10	259	1,089	282	40	4,341	1,310	5,687
11	514	1,159	596	41	9,765	1,115	10,888
12	567	1,021	579	42	13,465	1,456	19,605
13	585	975	570	43	1,840	1,407	2,589
14	1,242	989	1,228	44	750	1,215	912
15	1,765	976	1,723	45	4,418	1,223	5,403
16	2,120	647	1,372	46	344	928	319
17	7,006	883	6,187	47	487	924	450
18	2,523	734	1,852	48	841	954	802
19	1,832	581	1,064		137,535 (Total)	1,075 (Weighted average)	147,726 (Total)
20	3,744	980	3,669				
21	2,406	1,010	2,430				
22	2,707	968	2,621				
23	3,121	1,057	3,299				
24	8,043	1,308	10,520				
25	2,135	502	1,072				
26	2,893	631	1,826				
27	3,030	710	2,152				
28	2,750	658	1,810				
29	3,581	1,067	3,821				
30	5,679	1,180	6,702				

A. States—See Table IV and Figure 1.
B. Average Populations (in thousands) by States in the United States (1940–49).
C. Average Annual per Capita Income in Dollars by States in the United States (1940–49). (Weighted Average of Income Payments to Individuals.)
D. Economic Populations = $B \times C$.
SOURCES: See Appendix.

The number of individual distances between each individual and all other control points of course varies as to the square of the number of control points used.

Therefore, if the 3,050 counties plus the 53 separate and independent areas which are in no county but are of the order of county size had been used, these 3,103 control points would have occasioned the use of 9,928,909 distances!

Since the distance from point *A* to point *B* is the same as *B* to *A*, and so on for each pair, only half of the distances need be measured and the rest of the table may be

Table VIII

DISTANCES BETWEEN THE GEOGRAPHIC CENTERS OF STATES IN THE UNITED STATES (UNITS OF 100 STATUTE MILES)

A-1

	1	2	3	4	5	6	7	8	9	10	11	12
1 Wash.	x	2.5	8	6	4	7.5	10	11.5	9.5	7	5	9.5
2 Ore.	2.5	x	5	4	3	6	8	10	9	7	6	10
3 Calif.	8	5	x	2.5	6	5	5	8	8	8	9	12.5
4 Nev.	6	4	2.5	x	4	3	4.5	7	6.5	6	7	10.5
5 Idaho	4	3	6	4	x	4	7	8	6	3.5	3	7.5
6 Utah	7.5	6	5	3	4	x	3.5	4.5	3.5	3.5	5	8
7 Ariz.	10	8	5	4.5	7	3.5	x	3	5	6.5	9	11
8 N.M.	11.5	10	8	7	8	4.5	3	x	3	6	9	9.5
9 Colo.	9.5	9	8	6.5	6	3.5	5	3	x	3	6	6
10 Wyo.	7	7	8	6	3.5	3.5	6.5	6	3	x	3	4.5
11 Mont.	5	6	9	7	3	5	9	9	6	3	x	4
12 N. Dak	9.5	10	12.5	10.5	7.5	8	11	9.5	6	4.5	4	x
13 S. Dak	10	10	12	10	7.5	7	9.5	7.5	5	4	5	2
14 Nebr.	11	11	11.5	9.5	8	6.5	8	6	3.5	4	6	4
15 Kan.	13	12.5	12	10.5	9.5	7.5	8	5	4	6	8	6
16 Okla.	15	14	13	11.5	11	8.5	8	5	5	8	10	9
17 Tex.	16.5	15	13	12	12.5	9.5	8	5	7	10	12	11
18 La.	19	18	16.5	15.5	15	12.5	11.5	8.5	9	12	14	12
19 Ark.	17	16.5	15.5	14	13.5	11	11	8	8	10	12	10
20 Mo.	15.5	15.5	15	13.5	12	10.5	11	8	7	9	11	7.5
21 Iowa	14	14	15	12.5	11	10	11	9	7	7	9	5
22 Minn.	12.5	13	15	12.5	10	10	12	10	7.5	7	7	3
23 Wisc.	15	15.5	17	15	12	12	13.5	11	9	9	10	5.5
24 Ill.	16.5	16.5	17	15.5	13	12	13	10	8.5	10	11	7.5

SOURCES: See Appendix.

Table VIII (cont.)

A-2

	13	14	15	16	17	18	19	20	21	22	23	24
1	10	11	13	75	16.5	19	17	15.5	14	12.5	15	16.5
2	10	11	12.5	14	15	18	16.5	15.5	14	13	15.5	16.5
3	12	11.5	12	13	13	16.5	15.5	15	15	15	17	17
4	7.5	9.5	10.5	11.5	12	15.5	14	13.5	12.5	12.5	15	15
5	7	8	9.5	11	12.5	15	13	12	11	10	12	13
6	9.5	6.5	7.5	8.5	9.5	12.5	11	10.5	10	10	12	12
7	9.5	8	8	8	8	11.5	11	11	11	12	13	13
8	7.5	6	5	5	5	8.5	8	8	9	10	11	10.5
9	5	3.5	4	5	7	9	8	7	7	7.5	9	8
10	4	4	6	8	10	12	10	9	7	7	9	10
11	5	6	8	10	12	14	12	11	9	7	10	11
12	2	4	6	9	11	12	10	7	5	3	5.5	7.5
13	x	2	4	7	9.5	10.5	8	6	4	3	5	6
14	2	x	2	4	7	8	6	4	3	4	5.5	5.5
15	4	2	x	2	5	6	4	3	3.5	6	6	5
16	7	5	2	x	3	4	3	3.5	4	8	7.5	6
17	9.5	6	5	3	x	3.5	4	6	8	11	10.5	8
18	10.5	4	6	4	3.5	x	3	5	8	11	10	7
19	8	3	4	3	4	3	x	2	5	8	7	4
20	6	3.5	3	3.5	6	5	2	x	2.5	6	4.5	2
21	4	6	3.5	4	8	8	5	2.5	x	3	2.5	2.5
22	3	6	6	8	11	11	8	6	3	x	3	5
23	5	5	6	7.5	10.5	10	7	4.5	2.5	3	x	3
24	6	5.5	5	6	8	7	4	2	2.5	5	3	x

A-3

	25	26	27	28	29	30	31	32	33	34	35	36
1	19.5	20.5	20	20	18	18	20	21.5	22	25.5	23	23
2	19	20	19.5	19.5	18	18.5	20	21.5	22	25	23	23
3	17.5	19.5	19	19.5	18.5	19.5	20.5	22	21	23.5	22.5	23
4	16	18	17.5	17.5	16.5	17.5	18.5	22	19.5	22	21.5	21
5	15.5	17	16	16	15	15	16.5	18	19	21.5	19	20
6	13	15	14.5	14.5	14	14.5	15.5	17	17	19	18	18
7	13	15	15	15	15	16	16.5	17.5	16.5	18.5	18	19
8	10	11.5	11.5	12	12	13	13.5	15	13	15.5	15	15.5
9	10	11.5	11	11	10.5	11	12	13.5	13	16	14	15
10	12	14	12.5	12.5	11.5	12	13	15	15	18	16	16
11	14.5	16	14	13	13	12.5	14	16	17	20	18	18
12	12	12.5	11	10.5	9	8	10	12	14	17	14	14
13	10	11	9.5	9	8	8	9	11	12	15.5	13	13
14	8	9.5	8	8	7	8	9	10.5	11	14	12	12
15	6	8	7	7	7	8	8	9.5	9	12	10	11
16	5	7	6.5	7	7	9	9	8	10	11	10	11
17	5	7	8	9	9.5	11.5	11	12	9	11	11	12
18	2	4	5	6	7.5	10	9	9	6	7	7.5	9
19	2	4	4	5	5	7	7	7	6	8	7	8
20	4	5	4	4	4	5	5.5	7	7	10	7.5	8
21	7	7.5	6	6	4	5	6	7.5	9	12	9	9
22	10	10.5	8.5	8	6	5	7.5	9	11.5	15	11.5	11
23	8	8	6	5.5	3.5	3	4.5	6.5	9	12.5	9	9
24	5	5.5	3	3	1	3	3	5	6	10	7	7

SOURCES: See Appendix.

A-4

Table VIII (cont.)

	37	38	39	40	41	42	43	44	45	46	47	48
1	23	23	24	24	22	22	24	24.5	24	23.5	24	24
2	23	23	24	24	22.5	23	24.5	25.5	25	24	25	25.5
3	23	23.5	24.5	25	23	24	26	26.5	26	25.5	26	27
4	21	21.5	23	23	21	22	23.5	24	24	23.5	24	25
5	19.5	20	21	21	19	20	21.5	22	21.5	21	21.5	22.5
6	18	19	19.5	20	18	19.5	20.5	21.5	21	20 5	21	22
7	19	20	20 5	21	19	20.5	22	22 5	22	22	22.5	23.5
8	16	16.5	17.5	18	16	18	18	19.5	19.5	19	19.5	21
9	15	15	16	16.5	15	16	17.5	18	18	17	18	19
10	16	16	17	17	15.5	16.5	18	18.5	18	17.5	18	19
11	17	17.5	18.5	18.5	16.5	17	19	19 5	19	18	19	19.5
12	13	13	14	14	12	13	14.5	15	14.5	13.5	14.5	15
13	12	12	13	13.5	12	13.5	14	14.5	14	13.5	14	15
14	12	12	13	13	11.5	12.5	14	14	14.5	14	14.5	15.5
15	11	11.5	12	13	11	12.5	14	14	14	14	14	15.5
16	11	12	12.5	13	11.5	13	14	15	14.5	14	15	16
17	12	13.5	14	15	13.5	15.5	16	17	17	17	17	19
18	9.5	9.5	11	12	11	13.5	14	14	14	14	14.5	16
19	8	9	10	11	9	11	12	12	12	12	12.5	14
20	8	8	9	10	8	10	11	11.5	11	11	11.5	13
21	9	9	10	10	8	9.5	11	11.5	11	11	11	12
22	10.5	10.5	11.5	11	9	10	11.5	11.5	12	11	11.5	12
23	8	8	9	8.5	7	7.5	9	9.5	9	8.5	9	10
24	6	6.5	7.5	8	6	7.5	9	9	9	9	9	11

B-1

	1	2	3	4	5	6	7	8	9	10	11	12
25 Miss.	19.5	19	17.5	16	15.5	13	13	10	10	12	14.5	12
26 Ala.	20.5	20	19.5	18	17	15	15	11.5	11.5	14	16	12.5
27 Tenn.	20	19.5	19	17.5	16	14.5	15	11.5	11	12.5	14	11
28 Ky.	20	19.5	19.5	17.5	16	14.5	15	12	11	12.5	13	10.5
29 Ind.	18	18	18.5	16 5	15	14	15	12	10.5	11.5	13	9
30 Mich.	18	18.5	19.5	17.5	15	14.5	16	13	11	12	12.5	8
31 Ohio	20	20	20.5	18.5	16,5	15.5	16.5	13.5	12	13	14	10
32 W.Va.	21.5	21.5	22	20	18	17	17.5	15	13.5	15	16	12
33 Ga.	22	22	21	19.5	19	17	16.5	13	13	15	17	14
34 Fla.	25.5	25	23.5	22	21.5	19	18,5	15.5	16	18	20	17
35 S. Ca.	23	23	22.5	21	19.5	18	18	15	14	16	18	14
36 N. Ca.	23	23	23	21	20	18	19	15	15	16	18	14
37 Va.	23	23	23	21	19.5	18	19	16	15	16	17	13
38 Md.	23	23.5	23.5	21.5	20	19	20	16.5	15	16	17.5	13
39 Del.	24	24	24.5	23	21	19.5	20.5	17.5	16	17	18.5	14
40 N.J.	24	24	25	23	21	20	21	18	16.5	17	18.5	14
41 Pa.	22	22.5	23	21	19	18	19	16	15	15.5	16.5	12
42 N.Y.	22	23	24	22	20	19.5	20.5	18	16	16.5	17	13
43 Con.	24	24.5	26	23.5	21.5	20.5	22	18	17.5	18	19	14.5
44 R.I.	24.5	25.5	26.5	24	22	21.5	22.5	19,5	18	18.5	19.5	15
45 Mass.	24	25	26	24	21.5	21	22	19.5	18	18	19	14.5
46 Ver.	23.5	24	25.5	23.5	21	20.5	22	19	17	17.5	18	13.5
47 N.H.	24	25	26	24	21.5	21	22.5	19.5	18	18	19	14.5
48 Me.	24	25.5	27	25	22.5	22	23.5	21	19	19	19.5	15

SOURCES: See Appendix.

Table VIII (cont.)

B-2

	13	14	15	16	17	18	19	20	21	22	23	24
25	10	8	6	5	5	2	2	4	7	10	8	5
26	11	9.5	8	7	6	4	4	5	7.5	10.5	8	5.5
27	9.5	8	7	6.5	8	5	4	4	6	8.5	6	3
28	9	8	7	7	9	6	5	4	6	8	5.5	3
29	8	7	7	7	9.5	7.5	5	4	4	6	3.5	1
30	8	8	8	9	11.5	10	7	5	5	5	3	3
31	9	9	8	9	11	9	7	5.5	6	7.5	4.5	3
32	11	10.5	9.5	8	12	9	7	7	7.5	9	6.5	5
33	12	11	9	10	9	6	6	7	9	11.5	9	6
34	15.5	14	12	11	11	7	8	10	12	15	12.5	10
35	13	12	10	10	11	7.5	7	7.5	9	11.5	9	7
36	13	12	11	11	12	9	8	8	9	11	9	7
37	12	12	11	11	12	9.5	8	8	9	10.5	8	6
38	12	12	11.5	12	13.5	9.5	9	8	9	10.5	8	6.5
39	13	13	12	12.5	14	11	10	9	10	11.5	9	7.5
40	13.5	13	13	13	15	12	11	10	10	11	8.5	8
41	12	11.5	11	11.5	13.5	11	9	8	8	9	7	6
42	13.5	12.5	12.5	13	15.5	13.5	11	10	9.5	10	7.5	7.5
43	14	14	14	14	16	14	12	11	11	11.5	9	9
44	14.5	14	14	15	17	14	12	11.5	11.5	11.5	9.5	9
45	14	14.5	14	14.5	17	14	12	11	11	12	9	9
46	13.5	14	14	14	17	14	12	11	11	11	8.5	9
47	14	14.5	14	15	17	14.5	12.5	11.5	11	11.5	9	9
48	15	15.5	15.5	16	19	16	14	13	12	12	10	11

B-3

	25	26	27	28	29	30	31	32	33	34	35	36
25	x	2	2	4	5.5	8	7	7	4	6	5	6.5
26	2	x	2	3.5	5	7.5	6	5.5	2	4	4	5
27	3	2	x	1	3	5	3.5	3.5	3	6	3	4
28	4	3.5	1	x	2	4	2	3	3.5	7	3.5	3.5
29	5.5	5	3	2	x	2	2	3	6	9	5	5
30	8	7.5	5	4	2	x	2	4	7.5	11	7	6
31	7	6	3.5	2	2	2	x	1.5	5.5	9	5	4
32	7	5.5	3.5	3	3	4	1.5	x	4.5	7.5	3.5	2.5
33	4	2	3	3.5	6	7.5	5.5	4.5	x	3	1.5	3
34	6	4	6	7	9	11	9	7.5	3	x	4	6
35	5	4	3	3.5	5	7	5	3.5	1.5	4	x	1
36	6.5	5	4	3.5	5	6	4	2.5	3	6	1	x
37	7	6	4	3.5	4.5	5	3	1	4.5	7	3	1
38	8	7	5	4.5	5	5	3	2	6	7	4	3
39	9	8	6	5	6	6	4	3	6	9	4.5	3
40	10	9	7	6	6	6	4.5	3.5	7	10	6	4
41	9	8	6	5	4	4	2.5	2	7	9.5	5	4
42	11	10	7.5	6.5	6	5	4	4	7	11.5	7	6
43	11	10	8	7	7	6	5	5	8.5	11	7	5.5
44	12	10.5	9	8	8	7	6	5	8.5	11.5	7.5	6
45	12	11	9	8	7.5	6.5	6	5	9	12	7.5	6
46	12	11	9	8	7.5	6	5.5	5	10	12	8	7
47	12	11	9	8	8	6.5	6	6	10	12	8	7
48	14	13	11	10	9	8	7.5	7.5	12	14	10	8

SOURCES: See Appendix.

B-4

Table VIII (cont.)

	37	38	39	40	41	42	43	44	45	46	47	48
25	7	8	9	10	9	11	11	12	12	12	12	14
26	6	7	8	9	8	10	10	10.5	11	11	11	13
27	4	5	6	9	6	7.5	8	9	9	9	9	11
28	3.5	4.5	5	6	5	6.5	7	8	8	8	8	10
29	4.5	5	6	6	4	6	7	8	7.5	7.5	8	9
30	5	5	6	6	4	5	6	7	6.5	6	6.5	8
31	3	3	4	4.5	2.5	4	5	6	6	5.5	6	7.5
32	1	2	3	3.5	2	4	5	5	5	5	6	7.5
33	4.5	6	6	7	7	7	8.5	8.5	9	10	10	12
34	7	7	9	10	9.5	11.5	11	11.5	12	12	12	14
35	3	4	4.5	6	5	7	7	7.5	7.5	8	8	10
36	1	3	3	4	4	6	5.5	6	6	7	7	8
37	x	1	2	3	2	4	4	5	5	5	5	7
38	1	x	1	1	1	3	3	3	3.5	4	4	6
39	2	1	x	1	2	3	3	3	3	4	4	6
40	3	1	1	x	2	2	1	2	2	3	3	4
41	2	1	2	2	x	2	3	3	3	3	3	5
42	4	3	3	2	2	x	1.5	2	2	1	2	3
43	4	3	3	1	3	1.5	x	1	1	2	1.5	3
44	5	3	3	2	3	2	1	x	1	2	1	3
45	5	3.5	3	2	3	2	1	1	x	1	1	2
46	5	4	4	3	3	1	2	2	1	x	1	2
47	5	4	4	3	3	2	1.5	1	1	1	x	2
48	7	6	6	4	5	3	3	3	2	2	2	x

SOURCES: See Appendix.

filled in accordingly. But, since the values (population or commodity) can and do differ at *A* and *B* the computation of the total potential at each control point requires, then, a number of separate arithmetic divisions, the total of which would be the square of the number of control points.

For this study the use of county data was out of the realm of possibility. The state, then, was the smallest geographical area for which all the data required were available and which lent itself to the great amount of computational work involved.

To convert the production data into Time Potentials (i.e., Product Supply Time Potentials also described in

Chapter 2), the two time differences (past and future) between all the twelve months and each one in turn were required. All production occurring within a given month was assumed to be concentrated at mid-month. The middle of each month then was a time control point and the values of total potential calculated for each time control point furnished the basis for drawing a curve of Product Supply Time Potential. The production by month data (see Table III) was compiled from the tables containing harvest date(s) by state. (See Tables XI, XII, XIII, and XIV.) The actual time potential for any particular harvest date can be estimated readily from the values calculated for the time control points. Table IX contains the 288 time differences (past and future) between each month in turn and all other months that were used to compute the Product Supply Time Potential values used in this study.

To obtain the values required to carry out the multiple linear correlation, it was necessary to compute various potentials from the basic data just described.

Accordingly, Gross Economic Population Potential (GEPP) was calculated for each of the 48 state-centered control points. Table X contains the values so computed.

From these 48 "known" values a map (see Figure 2) was prepared using the isogram technique. Lines connecting points of equal value were drawn and these "contour" lines make considerably easier the perception of the geographical pattern of Gross Economic Population Potential. On the map itself the intensity of GEPP can be estimated for any point in the United States. Portraying GEPP by use of a map creates the correct impression of the space continuum in which this "demand" or income potential factor exists.

Table IX

TIME DIFFERENCES (PAST AND FUTURE) BETWEEN THE MIDDLES OF MONTHS

(*Time differences in one month units*)

	Jan.	*Feb.*	*Mar.*	*Apr.*	*May*	*June*	*July*	*Aug.*	*Sept.*	*Oct.*	*Nov.*	*Dec.*
Jan.	12 x 12	11 1	10 2	9 3	8 4	7 5	6 6	5 7	4 8	3 9	2 10	1 11
Feb.	1 11	12 x 12	11 1	10 2	9 3	8 4	7 5	6 6	5 7	4 8	3 9	2 10
Mar.	2 10	1 11	12 x 12	11 1	10 2	9 3	8 4	7 5	6 6	5 7	4 8	3 9
Apr.	3 9	2 10	1 11	12 x 12	11 1	10 2	9 3	8 4	7 5	6 6	5 7	4 8
May	4 8	3 9	2 10	1 11	12 x 12	11 1	10 2	9 3	8 4	7 5	6 6	5 7

June	5	4	3	2	1	12	11	10	9	8	7	6
						x						
	7	8	9	10	11	12	1	2	3	4	5	6
July	6	5	4	3	2	1	12	11	10	9	8	7
							x					
	6	7	8	9	10	11	12	1	2	3	4	5
Aug.	7	6	5	4	3	2	1	12	11	10	9	8
								x				
	5	6	7	8	9	10	11	12	1	2	3	4
Sept.	8	7	6	5	4	3	2	1	12	11	10	9
									x			
	4	5	6	7	8	9	10	11	12	1	2	3
Oct.	9	8	7	6	5	4	3	2	1	12	11	10
										x		
	3	4	5	6	7	8	9	10	11	12	1	2
Nov.	10	9	8	7	6	5	4	3	2	1	12	11
											x	
	2	3	4	5	6	7	8	9	10	11	12	1
Dec.	11	10	9	8	7	6	5	4	3	2	1	12
												x
	1	2	3	4	5	6	7	8	9	10	11	12

Table X

UNITED STATES—GROSS ECONOMIC POPULATION POTENTIAL BY STATES

(1940–49 AVERAGE)

State-GEPP		State-GEPP		State-GEPP		State-GEPP	
		Billions of dollars per 100 miles					
1	12.2	13	17.6	25	22.3	37	38.3
2	12.4	14	19.6	26	22.9	38	47.0
3	20.5	15	20.9	27	29.7	39	38.4
4	14.2	16	20.1	28	33.3	40	43.2
5	12.6	17	20.2	29	41.9	41	47.2
6	13.7	18	19.0	30	35.3	42	46.9
7	12.7	19	23.3	31	41.4	43	43.9
8	14.0	20	28.9	32	39 0	44	37.0
9	15.8	21	26.0	33	24.0	45	37.3
10	14.0	22	20.8	34	16.7	46	44.4
11	12.9	23	27.0	35	26.1	47	35.1
12	15.9	24	38.3	36	29.4	48	24.0

SOURCES: See Appendix.

The "supply" factor also exists in a space continuum. Therefore, Product Supply Space Potential values were computed for each of the 48 control points for wheat, potatoes, onions, and strawberries. Even though there was no production of a given commodity at certain control points, the supply potential created at those points was nevertheless calculated because the values were to be used subsequently. Figures 3, 4, 5, and 6 are maps of Product Supply Space Potentials constructed once again by using the "known" spot values and the isogram method.

The significantly different geographies of production result in substantially different contours on each of the Supply Space Potential maps.

The Product Supply Time Potential graphs as they were developed for each commodity are also included. See Figures 7, 8, 9, and 10.

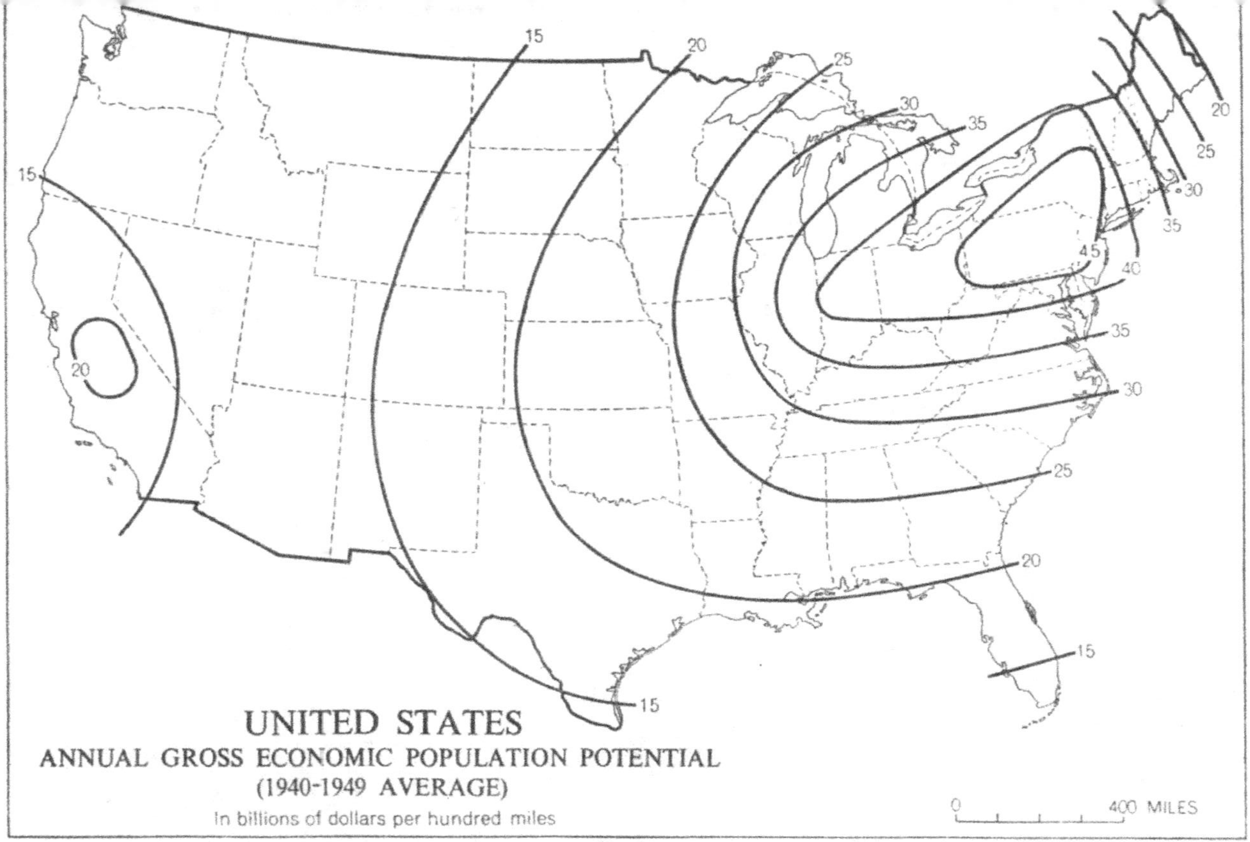
UNITED STATES
ANNUAL GROSS ECONOMIC POPULATION POTENTIAL
(1940-1949 AVERAGE)
In billions of dollars per hundred miles
0
400 MILES
15
20
25
30
35
40
45

Fig. 2

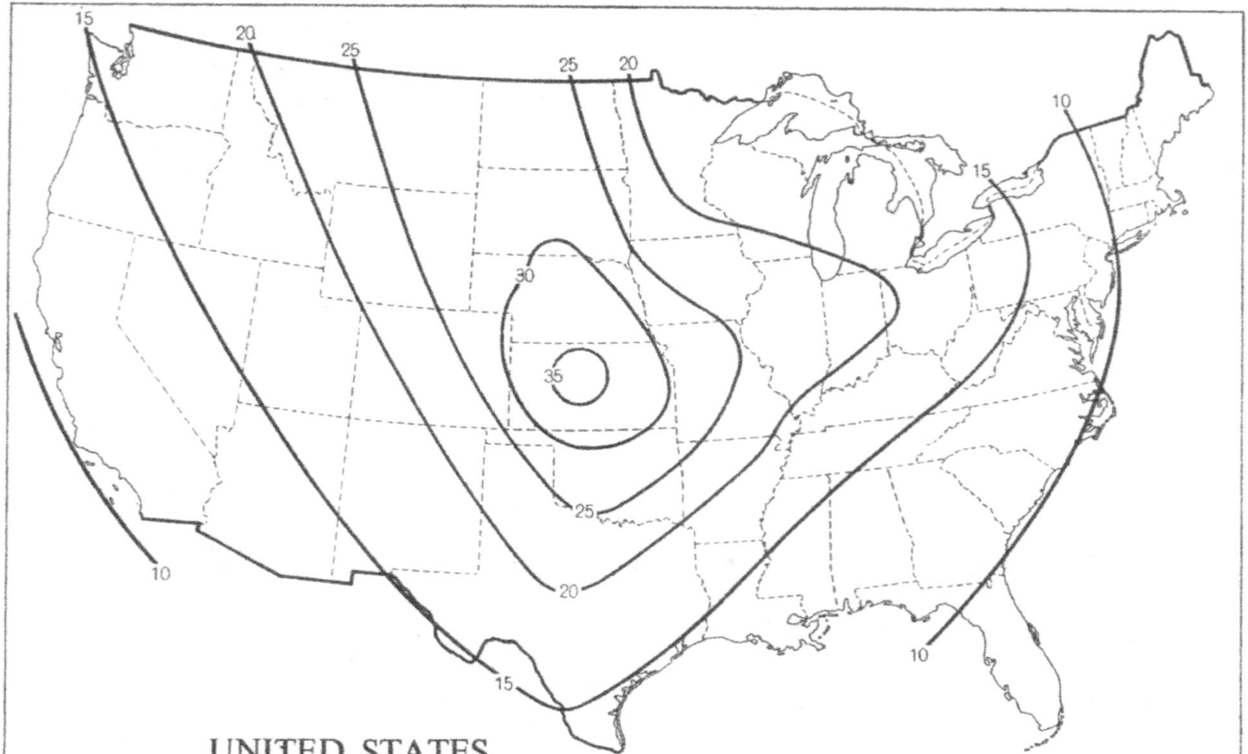

UNITED STATES
ANNUAL WHEAT SUPPLY SPACE POTENTIAL
(1940-1949 AVERAGE)

In tens of millions of bushels per hundred miles

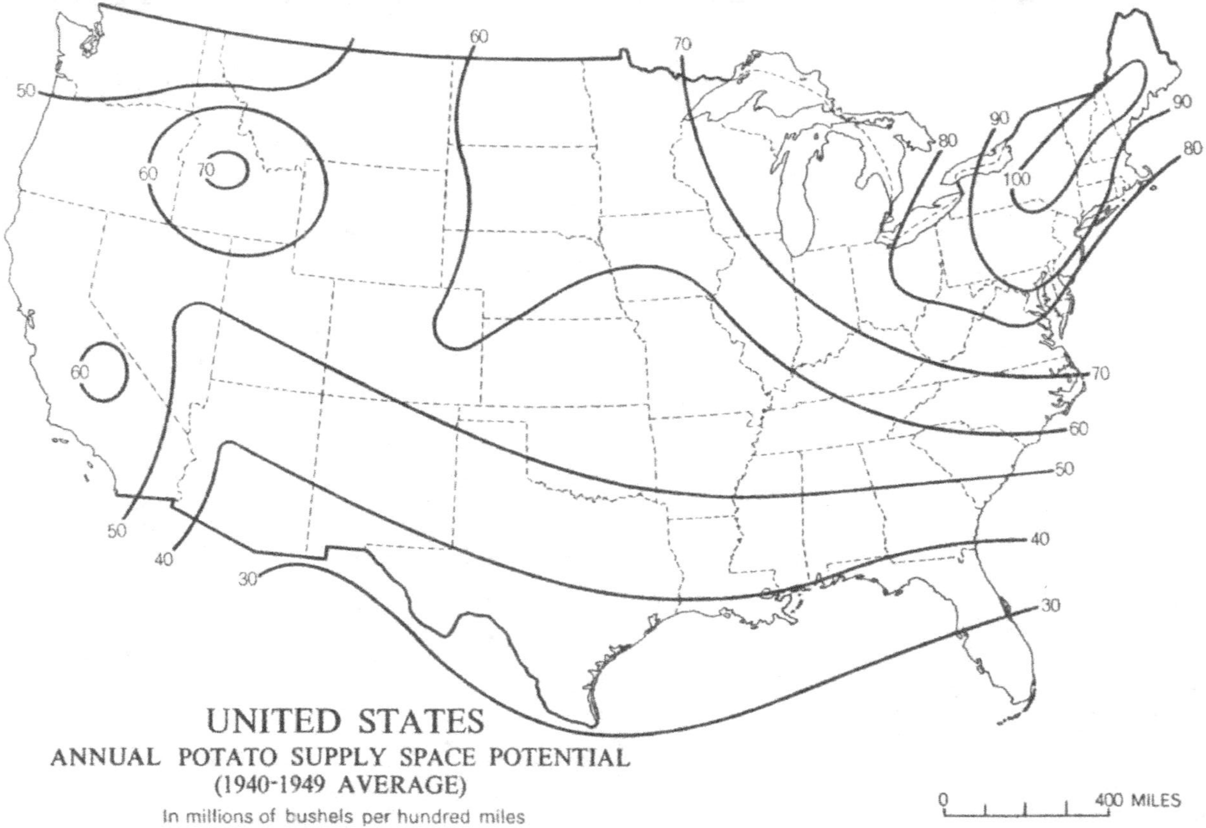

UNITED STATES
ANNUAL POTATO SUPPLY SPACE POTENTIAL
(1940-1949 AVERAGE)
In millions of bushels per hundred miles

Fig. 4

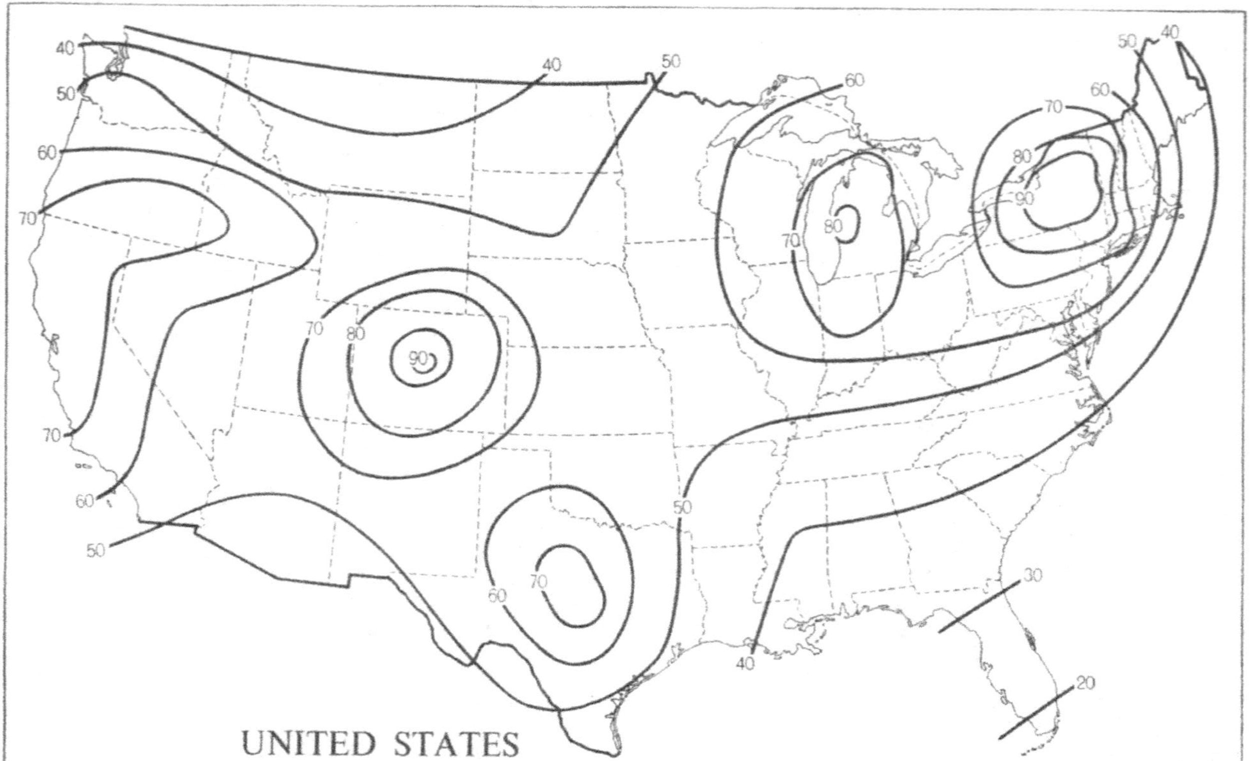

UNITED STATES
ANNUAL ONION SUPPLY SPACE POTENTIAL
(1940-1949 AVERAGE)
In hundreds of thousands of sacks (fifty pounds each) per hundred miles

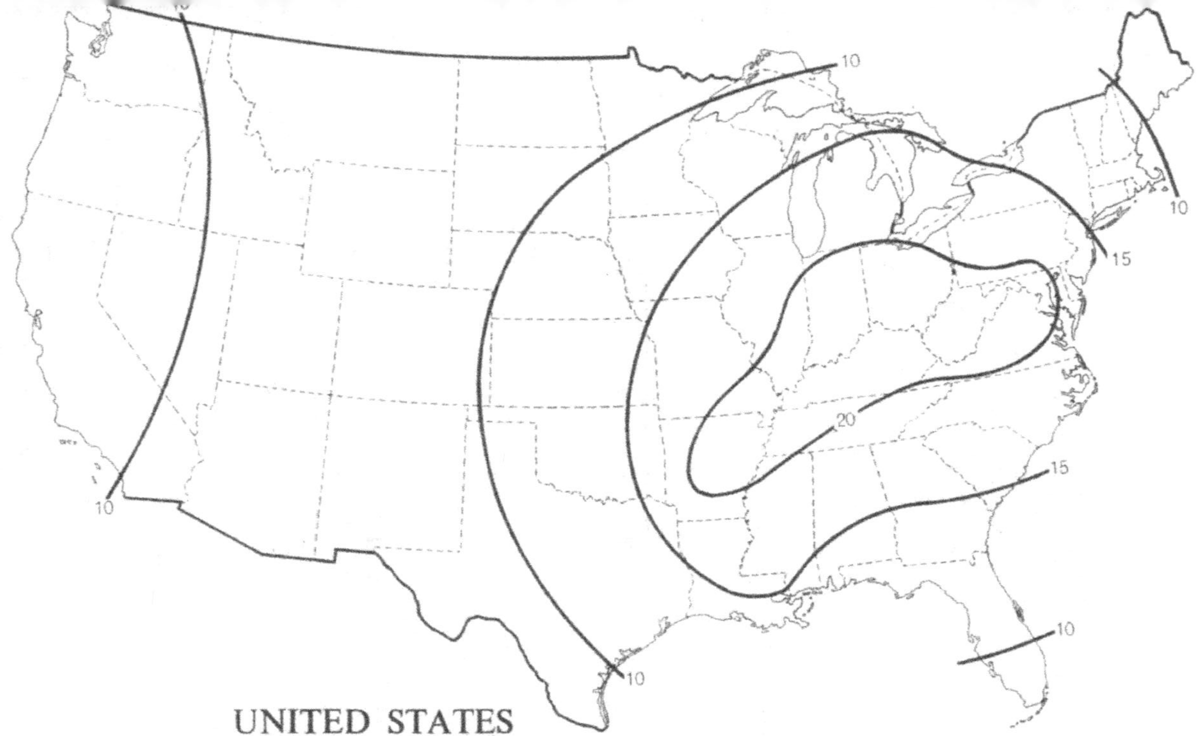

UNITED STATES

ANNUAL STRAWBERRY SUPPLY SPACE POTENTIAL
(1940-1949 AVERAGE)

0 400 MILES

In hundreds of thousands of crates (twenty four quarts each) per hundred miles

Fig. 6

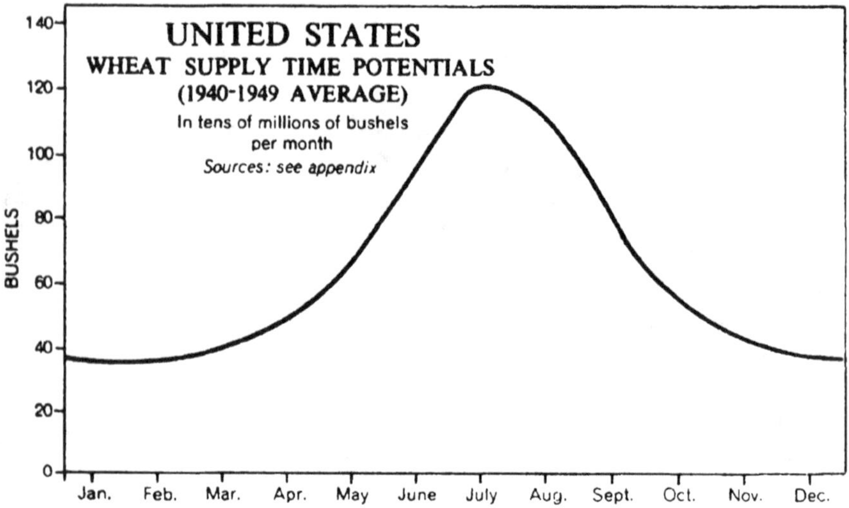
UNITED STATES
WHEAT SUPPLY TIME POTENTIALS
(1940-1949 AVERAGE)
In tens of millions of bushels per month
Sources: see appendix
BUSHELS
0
20
40
60
80
100
120
140
Jan.
Feb.
Mar.
Apr.
May
June
July
Aug.
Sept.
Oct.
Nov.
Dec.

Fig 7

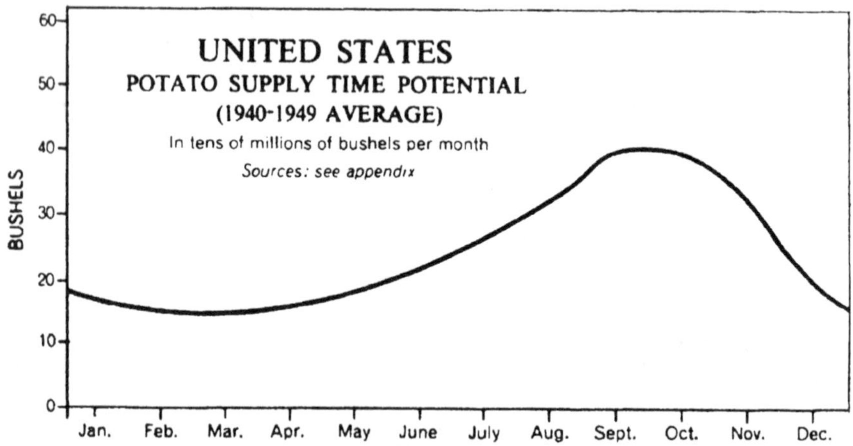
UNITED STATES
POTATO SUPPLY TIME POTENTIAL
(1940-1949 AVERAGE)
In tens of millions of bushels per month
Sources: see appendix
BUSHELS
0
10
20
30
40
50
60
Jan.
Feb.
Mar.
Apr.
May
June
July
Aug.
Sept.
Oct.
Nov.
Dec.

Fig 8

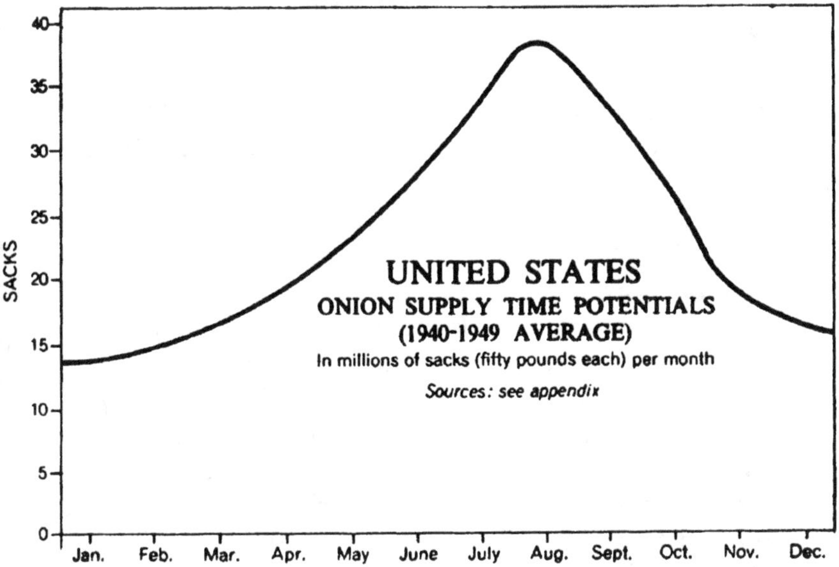

SACKS
40
35
30
25
20
15
10
5
0
UNITED STATES
ONION SUPPLY TIME POTENTIALS
(1940-1949 AVERAGE)
In millions of sacks (fifty pounds each) per month
Sources: see appendix
Jan.
Feb.
Mar.
Apr.
May
June
July
Aug.
Sept.
Oct.
Nov.
Dec.

Fig. 9

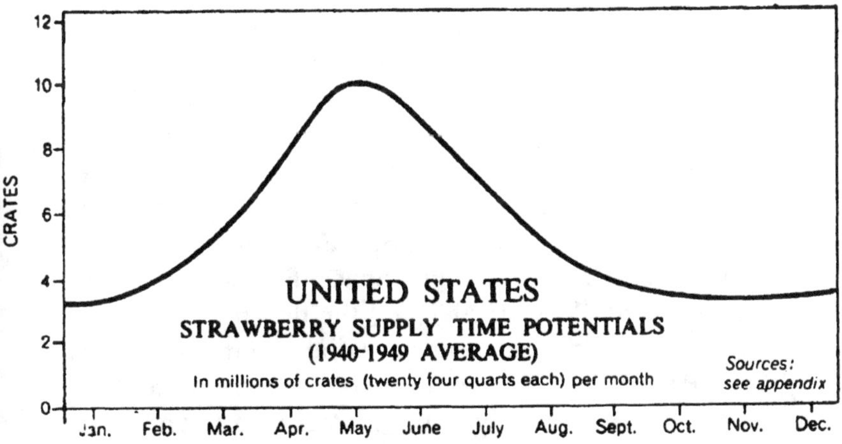

CRATES
12
10
8
6
4
2
0
UNITED STATES
STRAWBERRY SUPPLY TIME POTENTIALS
(1940-1949 AVERAGE)
In millions of crates (twenty four quarts each) per month
Sources: see appendix
Jan.
Feb.
Mar.
Apr.
May
June
July
Aug.
Sept.
Oct.
Nov.
Dec.

Fig. 10

To compute the various potential values at the control points and, subsequently, to test their influence on farm price, the following data were required (as previously indicated) in addition to time and space differences: production, farm prices, and harvest dates. Tables XI, XII, XIII, and XIV summarize these basic data for the commodities used.

It will be recalled that the data on these tables and those of time differences and distances were utilized to compute space and time potentials.

In the multiple correlation analysis used to test the hypothesis that the geographical variation of farm price of a commodity is a function of the concomitant geographical variation of Gross Economic Population Potential, Product Supply Space Potential, and Product Supply Time Potential, each of these variables was given a separate designation, i.e., X_1, X_2, X_3, and X_4. Tables XV, XVI, XVII, and XVIII present the data used in the multiple correlation in this manner for each of the four commodities.

Using the contour method to portray the geographical variation of a factor permits one to estimate the value of that factor at any point and would permit the escape from using only control point values in the analysis. Hence, the number of points of association used to test an hypothesis could be infinite. Theoretically, then, any number of evenly distributed geographical points might be used. Such would be the case of Gross Economic Population Potential or Product Supply Space Potential. But the variable being "explained," i.e., the dependent variable farm price, and the independent variable, Product Supply Time Potential, were not available in this form, their values being known only at the control points. Therefore, the number of observations utilized in the multiple cor-

UNITED STATES—WHEAT PRODUCTION, FARM PRICES, AND HARVEST DATES (1940–49 AVERAGES) BY STATES

A	B	C	D	A	B	C	D
State	*Production*	*Farm Price*	*Harvest Date*	*State*	*Production*	*Farm Price*	*Harvest Date*
1	61,580	144	8–5	33	2,470	163	6–7
2	22,666	147	7–25	34	—	—	—
3	10,969	161	7–1	35	3,135	168	6–8
4	529	149	8–13	36	6,801	171	6–16
5	31,154	139	8–6	37	8,117	166	6–27
6	6,937	141	7–29	38	6,840	163	7–1
7	575	165	6–1	39	1,231	165	6–26
8	4,176	144	7–22	40	1,440	163	7–7
9	35,996	145	7–17	41	18,440	161	7–4
10	4,976	142	8–1	42	8,367	162	7–23
11	68,845	145	8–8	43	4	—	—
12	137,943	155	8–15	44	2	—	—
13	41,358	152	8–5	45	6	—	—
14	63,652	150	7–11	46	3	—	—
15	193,512	150	7–1	47	1	—	—
16	73,998	147	6–21	48	26	—	—
17	63,486	146	6–25		1,071,347 (Total)	151 (Weighted average)	
18	18	—	—				
19	389	151	6–26				
20	22,658	154	6–29				
21	4,387	152	7–7				
22	22,004	157	8–9				
23	1,912	152	8–3				
24	28,879	156	7–2				
25	278	155	6–10				
26	200	164	6–12				
27	4,762	166	6–16				
28	5,401	161	6–21				
29	29,529	159	7–7				
30	23,553	161	7–18				
31	46,592	159	7–8				
32	1,550	164	7–2				

A. State—See Table IV and Figure 1.
B. Average Annual Production (1940–49) in thousands of bushels.
C. Average Farm Price (1940–49) in cents per bushel.
D. Date when Harvest is at peak (month and day).
SOURCES: See Appendix.

UNITED STATES—POTATO PRODUCTION, FARM PRICES, AND HARVEST DATES BY STATES (1940–49 AVERAGES)

A State	*B* Production	*C* Farm Price	*D* Harvest Date	*A* State	*B* Production	*C* Farm Price	*D* Harvest Date
1	9,524	128	10–16	33	1,517	152	6–1
2	10,736	136	10–8	34	4,306	181	3–15
3	21,549	128	6–3	35	2,457	150	5–24
4	524	144	10–16	36	9,295	127	6–20
5	37,379	94	10–15	37	8,998	133	7–5
6	2,801	127	10–11	38	1,906	138	7–18
7	1,179	158	8–8	39	342	148	8–5
8	283	—	9–20	40	11,213	121	8–23
9	17,313	121	10–16	41	19,176	144	9–23
10	2,219	130	10–3	42	32,145	130	9–22
11	2,100	138	9–1	43	3,440	—	10–8
12	19,589	103	9–23	44	1,263	—	10–8
13	2,435	138	9–25	45	3,214	—	10–8
14	10,542	110	10–3	46	1,430	—	10–7
15	1,824	115	7–3	47	1,102	—	10–7
16	1,540	133	6–14	48	59,654	109	10–1
17	4,648	160	4–1	3b	12,490	143	8–1
18	2,346	140	5–18		410,475 (Total)	122 (Weighted average)	
19	3,100	134	6–18				
20	3,446	126	7–15				
21	3,232	—	9–2				
22	18,147	111	9–25				
23	12,708	126	9–15				
24	1,981	—	10–2				
25	1,632	143	6–5				
26	4,186	129	5–15				
27	3,088	135	7–1				
28	3,546	138	7–15				
29	4,502	—	10–8				
30	17,755	126	10–10				
31	7,731	—	10–5				
32	2,042	—	9–20				

A. State—See Table IV and Figure 1.

B. Average Annual Production (1940–49) in thousands of bushels.

C. Average Farm Price (1940–49) in cents per bushel.

D. Date when Harvest is at Peak (month and day).

SOURCES: See Appendix.

A State	B Production	C Farm Price	D Harvest Date	A State	B Production	C Farm Price	D Harvest Date
1a	296	100	7–4	33	167	161	5–15
2	2,565	106	9–15	34	—	—	—
3a	1,484	150	5–15	35	—	—	—
4	217	125	8–15	36	—	—	—
5	2,078	74	9–1	37	79	165	7–1
6	646	117	9–15	38	—	—	—
7a	284	192	5–15	39	—	—	—
8	266	169	6–20	40	664	155	7–1
9	5,186	102	9–15	41	98	160	8–15
10	—	—	—	42	6,593	152	7–4
11	—	—	—	43	—	—	—
12	—	—	—	44	—	—	—
13	—	—	—	45	575	123	8–15
14	—	—	—	46	—	—	—
15	87	132	8–15	47	—	—	—
16	98	108	7–25	48	—	—	—
17a	4,822	174	4–5	1b	553	93	9–1
18	161	181	4–20	3b	541	125	7–1
19	—	—	—	3c	2,508	119	8–15
20	—	—	—	7b	55	106	8–15
21a	136	135	7–15	17b	1,076	164	5–25
22	1,563	125	9–5	21b	196	116	8–15
23	744	133	8–20		37,892 (Total)	131 (Weighted average)	
24	719	131	8–1				
25	—	—	—				
26	—	—	—				
27	—	—	—				
28	19	140	7–1				
29	882	139	8–26				
30	3,459	142	8–15				
31	365	163	9–1				
32	—	—	—				

A. State—See Table IV and Figure 1.

B. Average Annual Production (1940–49) in thousands of sacks (50 lbs. each).

C. Average Farm Price (1940–49) in cents per sack (50 lbs. each).

D. Time when Harvest is at Peak, month and day.

SOURCES: See Appendix.

Table XIV

UNITED STATES—STRAWBERRY PRODUCTION, FARM PRICES, AND HARVEST DATES BY STATES (1940–49 AVERAGES)

A State	B Production	C Farm Price	D Harvest Date	A State	B Production	C Farm Price	D Harvest Date
1	614	560	6–20	33	1	—	5–14
2	949	542	6–13	34	258	924	2–15
3a	223	864	4–10	35	24	687	5–1
4	—	—	—	36	314	664	5–7
5	—	—	—	37	333	570	5–18
6	57	884	6–5	38	228	615	5–27
7	—	—	—	39	84	608	6–4
8	—	—	—	40	188	670	6–10
9	—	—	—	41	168	718	6–12
10	—	—	—	42	312	739	6–23
11	—	—	—	43	—	—	—
12	—	—	—	44	—	—	—
13	—	—	—	45	—	—	—
14	—	—	—	46	—	—	—
15	65	561	6–3	47	—	—	—
16	72	539	5–18	48	—	—	—
17	56	741	4–8	3b	415	772	6–8
18	931	780	4–10		8,964 (Total)	636 (Weighted average)	
19	748	541	5–13				
20	236	645	6–5				
21	54	668	6–12				
22	—	—	—				
23	168	626	6–30				
24	182	602	6–6				
25	7	—	5–7				
26	183	520	4–20				
27	586	522	5–15				
28	316	610	6–2				
29	153	662	6–22				
30	703	632	6–25				
31	[illegible]	606	[illegible]				

A. State—See Table IV and Figure 1.
B. Average Annual Production (1940–49) in thousands of crates (24 quarts each).
C. Average Farm Price (1940–49) in cents per crate (24 quarts each).
D. Time when Harvest is at Peak, month and day.
SOURCES: See Appendix.

UNITED STATES—WHEAT SUPPLY SPACE AND SUPPLY TIME POTENTIALS, FARM PRICES, AND GROSS ECONOMIC POPULATION POTENTIALS BY STATES (1940–49)

State	X_1 Price	X_2 GEPP	X_3 PSSP	X_4 PSTP	State	X_1 Price	X_2 GEPP	X_3 PSSP	X_4 PSTP
1	144	12.2	16.5	11.5	32	164	39.0	16.2	11.3
2	147	12.4	14.0	11.9	33	163	24.0	11.7	9.2
3	161	20.5	10.3	11.1	34	—	(16.7)	(8.3)	—
4	149	14.2	11.8	11.2	35	168	26.1	11.8	9.4
5	139	12.6	17.3	11.5	36	171	29.4	12.3	10.2
6	141	13.7	14.2	11.8	37	166	38.3	13.9	11.0
7	165	12.7	11.7	8.5	38	163	47.0	14.2	11.1
8	144	14.0	15.7	12.0	39	165	38.4	11.8	10.9
9	145	15.8	21.4	12.1	40	163	43.2	11.3	11.5
10	142	14.0	19.2	11.7	41	161	47.1	14.6	11.4
11	145	12.9	21.6	11.4	42	162	46.9	11.4	11.9
12	155	15.9	29.2	11.1	43	—	(43.9)	(9.9)	—
13	152	17.6	28.0	11.5	44	—	(37.0)	(9.0)	—
14	150	19.6	31.5	12.0	45	—	(37.3)	(9.0)	—
15	150	20.9	37.8	11.1	46	—	(44.4)	(9.7)	—
16	147	20.1	28.7	10.5	47	—	(35.1)	(9.2)	—
17	146	20.2	20.3	10.8	48	—	(24.0)	(7.9)	—
18	—	(19.0)	(14.1)	—					
19	151	23.3	18.7	10.9					
20	154	28.9	23.3	11.1					
21	152	26.0	22.7	11.5					
22	157	20.8	20.7	11.3					
23	152	27.0	17.6	11.6					
24	156	38.3	23.4	11.3					
25	155	22.3	14.1	9.6					
26	164	22.9	12.4	99					
27	166	29.7	15.7	10.2					
28	161	33.3	17.4	10.5					
29	156	41.9	21.3	11.5					
30	161	35.3	18.2	12.1					
31	159	41.4	19.3	11.7					

State—See Table IV and Figure 1.

X_1—Price—Average Farm Price (1940–49) in cents per bushel.

X_2—Gross Economic Population Potential—Annual Average (1940–49) in billions of dollars per 100 miles.

X_3—Product Supply Space Potential—Annual Average (1940–49) in tens of millions of bushels per 100 miles.

X_4—Product Supply Time Potential—Annual Average (1940–49) in hundreds of millions of bushels per month.

SOURCES: See Appendix.

Table XVI

UNITED STATES—POTATO SUPPLY SPACE AND SUPPLY TIME POTENTIALS, FARM PRICES, AND GROSS ECONOMIC POPULATION POTENTIALS BY STATES (1940–49)

State	X_1 Price	X_2 GEPP	X_3 PSSP	X_4 PSTP	State	X_1 Price	X_2 GEPP	X_3 PSSP	X_4 PSTP
1	128	12.2	46.9	39.1	32	—	(39.0)	(79.4)	—
2	136	12.4	53.1	39.5	33	152	24.0	49.8	20.9
3a	128	20.5	62.3	21.0	34	181	16.7	27.5	15.1
4	144	14.2	49.0	39.1	35	150	26.1	58.4	20.0
5	94	12.6	73.6	39.2	36	127	29.4	68.6	22.5
6	127	13.7	49.2	39.3	37	133	38.3	80.5	24.5
7	158	12.7	39.4	30.7	38	138	47.0	94.8	26.3
8	—	(14.0)	(41.4)	—	39	148	38.4	77.5	30.0
9	121	15.8	59.6	39.1	40	121	43.2	87.9	35.2
10	130	14.0	54.6	37.6	41	144	47.1	93.4	40.3
11	138	15.8	51.8	36.3	42	130	46.9	101.5	40.2
12	103	14.0	64.9	40.1	43	—	(43.9)	(93.5)	—
13	138	12.9	61.4	36.4	44	—	(37.0)	(81.0)	—
14	110	15.9	62.1	37.6	45	—	(37.3)	(92.0)	—
15	115	20.9	53.7	25.6	46	—	(44.4)	(104.3)	—
16	133	20.1	53.8	22.0	47	—	(35.1)	(88.5)	—
17	160	20.2	40.3	15.5	48	109	24.0	101.7	40.0
18	140	19.0	42.1	19.5	3b	143	20.5	62.3	28.5
19	134	23.3	51.1	22.3					
20	126	28.9	56.7	25.7					
21	—	(26.0)	(60.0)	—					
22	111	20.8	67.8	40.1					
23	126	27.0	72.4	40.5					
24	—	(38.3)	(65.6)	—					
25	143	23.3	48.9	21.1					
26	129	22.9	48.6	20.5					
27	135	29.7	59.2	23.5					
28	138	33.3	64.7	25.7					
29	—	(41.9)	(71.7)	—					
30	126	35.3	76.9	39.9					

State—See Table IV and Figure 1.

X_1—Price—Farm Price (1940–49 average) in cents per bushel.

X_2—Gross Economic Population Potential—Annual Average (1940–49) in billions of dollars per 100 miles.

X_3—Product Supply Space Potential—Annual Average (1940–49) in millions of bushels per 100 miles.

X_4—Product Supply Time Potential—Annual Average (1940–49) in tens of millions of bushels per month.

SOURCES: See Appendix.

POPULATION POTENTIALS BY STATES (1940–49)

State	X_1 Price	X_2 GEPP	X_3 PSSP	X_4 PSTP	State	X_1 Price	X_2 GEPP	X_3 PSSP	X_4 PSTP
1a	100	12.2	48.7	29.2	34	—	(16.7)	(27.9)	—
2	106	12.4	65.0	33.0	35	—	(26.1)	(37.8)	—
3a	150	20.5	76.5	22.1	36	—	(29.4)	(40.4)	—
4	125	14.2	57.8	37.2	37	165	38.3	48.8	29.0
5	74	12.6	65.0	35.1	38	—	(47.0)	(58.8)	—
6	117	13.7	59.2	33.0	39	—	(38.4)	(55.3)	—
7a	192	12.7	49.2	22.1	40	155	43.2	66.7	29.0
8	169	14.0	56.3	27.1	41	160	47.1	69.4	37.2
9	102	15.8	89.6	33.0	42	152	46.9	98.6	29.2
10	—	(14.0)	(55.3)	—	43	—	(43.9)	(79.2)	—
11	—	(15.8)	(41.4)	—	44	—	(37.0)	(63.3)	—
12	—	(14.0)	(44.1)	—	45	123	37.3	63.8	37.2
13	—	(12.9)	(48.4)	—	46	—	(44.4)	(96.2)	—
14	—	(15.9)	(54.5)	—	47	—	(35.1)	(62.7)	—
15	132	20.9	53.8	37.2	48	—	(24.0)	(45.8)	—
16	108	20.1	54.8	33.5	1b	93	12.2	48.7	35.1
17a	174	20.2	78.9	19.0	3b	125	20.5	76.5	29.0
18	181	19.0	43.8	20.0	3c	119	20.5	76.5	37.2
19	—	(23.3)	(47.2)	—	7b	106	12.7	49.2	37.2
20	—	(28.9)	(51.9)	—	16b	164	20.2	78.9	23.5
21a	135	26.0	55.6	31.7	21b	116	26.0	55.6	37.2
22	125	20.8	58.6	34.3					
23	133	27.0	60.5	36.7					
24	131	38.3	66.8	34.1					
25	—	(23.3)	(39.0)	—					
26	—	(22.9)	(39.3)	—					
27	—	(29.7)	(46.0)	—					
28	140	33.3	51.2	29.0					
29	139	41.9	71.7	36.0					
30	142	35.3	81.2	37.2					
31	163	41.4	67.3	35.1					
32	—	(39.0)	(53.9)	—					
33	161	24.0	39.1	22.0					

State—See Table IV and Figure 1.

X_1—Price—Farm Price (1940–49 average) in cents per sack (50 lbs. each).

X_2—Gross Economic Population Potential—Annual Average (1940–49) in billions of dollars per 100 miles.

X_3—Product Supply Space Potential—Annual Average (1940–49) in hundreds of thousands of sacks (50 lbs. each) per 100 miles.

X_4—Product Supply Time Potential—Annual Average (1940–49) in millions of sacks (50 lbs. each) per month.

SOURCES: See Appendix.

Table XVIII

UNITED STATES—STRAWBERRY SUPPLY SPACE AND SUPPLY TIME POTENTIALS, FARM PRICES, AND GROSS ECONOMIC POPULATION POTENTIALS BY STATES (1940–49)

State	X_1 Price	X_2 GEPP	X_3 PSSP	X_4 PSTP	X_1 State	X_2 Price	X_3 GEPP	X_4 PSSP	PSTP
1	560	12.2	14.3	8.9	32	—	(39.0)	(19.9)	—
2	542	12.4	16.8	9.2	33	—	(24.0)	(14.7)	—
3	864	20.5	12.3	7.0	34	924	16.7	11.6	3.7
4	—	(14.2)	(10.0)	—	35	687	26.1	16.4	8.5
5	—	(12.6)	(10.1)	—	36	664	29.4	18.4	9.0
6	884	13.7	9.0	9.4	37	570	38.3	21.1	9.7
7	—	(12.7)	(7.9)	—	38	615	47.0	21.0	9.5
8	—	(14.0)	(8.5)	—	39	608	38.4	17.3	9.4
9	—	(15.8)	(9.1)	—	40	670	43.2	16.4	9.3
10	—	(14.0)	(8.6)	—	41	718	47.1	18.4	9.2
11	—	(15.8)	(8.4)	—	42	739	46.9	14.5	8.7
12	—	(14.0)	(8.6)	—	43	—	(43.9)	(13.5)	—
13	—	(12.9)	(9.4)	—	44	—	(37.0)	(11.3)	—
14	—	(15,9)	(10.7)	—	45	—	(37.3)	(11.5)	—
15	561	20.9	12.5	9.4	46	—	(44.4)	(12.5)	—
16	539	20.1	12.8	9.7	47	—	(35.1)	(10.7)	—
17	741	20.2	11.7	6.9	48	—	(24.0)	(7.6)	—
18	780	19.0	19.8	7.0	3b	772	20.5	12.3	9.3
19	541	23.3	20.9	9.5					
20	645	28.9	18.5	9.4					
21	668	26.0	13.6	9.2					
22	—	(20.8)	(10.3)	—					
23	626	27.0	14.1	8.3					
24	602	38.3	19.4	9.3					
25	—	(23.3)	(19.9)	—					
26	520	22.9	17.1	7.7					
27	522	29.7	22 9	9.7					
28	610	33.3	23.4	9.5					
29	662	41.9	21.0	8.9					
30	632	35.3	19.8	8.6					

State—See Table IV and Figure 1.

X_1—Price—Farm Price (1940–49 average) in cents per crate (24 quarts each).

X_2—Gross Economic Population Potential—Annual Average (1940–49) in billions of dollars per 100 miles.

X_3—Product Supply Space Potential—Annual Average (1940–49) in hundred of thousands of crates (24 quarts each) per 100 miles.

X_4—Product Supply Time Potential—Annual Average (1940–49) in millions of crates (24 quarts each) per month.

relation analysis of each individual commodity depended upon the number of control points for which values for all four variables were available. Obviously, if no production occurred at a control point, then farm price and harvest date were not available. With no harvest date then no time potential could be computed. However, Product Supply Space Potential does exist and can be calculated for a control point regardless of whether there is or is not production at that point. Since PSSP and GEPP values are subsequently utilized together for all control points (see Chapter 4) they are included in parentheses in Tables XV, XVI, XVII, and XVIII although the control point associations which could be utilized in the multiple correlation were restricted to those which had values for all four variables. The number of grouped observations varied from 29 for strawberries to 40 for wheat. For onions 33 were available and for potatoes 38. The significance of this number of observations and the number of constants (or variables since the two totals are the same in linear correlation) was discussed previously. (See Part *A* of this chapter.)

4

Summary of Results, Further Applications, and Conclusions of the Concepts and Techniques Developed

A. Results Summarized

THE multiple correlation, as outlined in Part *A* of Chapter 3, using the concepts developed in Chapter 2, with actual values developed in Part *B* of Chapter 3, was duly carried out for wheat, potatoes, onions, and strawberries.

Before beginning any discussion of the results, it might be well to summarize these results. Table XIX contains this summary of computations.

The coefficients of correlation, $R_{1.234}$, as found by multiple linear correlation, range from .87 for wheat to .72 for potatoes with the value for onions being .81 and that for strawberries .73. All these values seem to be significantly high so as to permit an acceptance of the hypothesis of this study. But "significantly" is a word that is of little meaning unless one insists upon a measure of it. The computed *R* values indicate the correlation in the data actually used. But, as was previously indicated, these values are affected by the number of grouped observations used as well as the number of degrees of freedom lost by reason of the type of estimating equation used. Hence, $\bar{R}_{1.234}$ was computed in a manner described in Chapter 3, and is considered as the best estimate of the coefficient of multiple correlation for the statistical universe from which the data used were drawn.

Table XIX

SUMMARY OF RESULTS, MULTIPLE LINEAR CORRELATION ANALYSIS-COMPETED VALUES

Measures Computed	*Commodities*			
	Wheat	*Potatoes*	*Onions*	*Strawberries*
$R_{1\cdot 234}$	.87	.72	.81	.73
$S_{1\cdot 234}$	\$.04	\$.11	\$.16	\$.72
$b_{12\cdot 34}$	.5074	1.2651	1.3164	3.2057
$b_{13\cdot 24}$	−.1705	−.9541	−.2624	−13.5313
$b_{14\cdot 23}$	−5.3095	−.1061	−3.4805	−47.5345
$d^2_{12\cdot 34}$	.4379	.0436	.2000	−.0423
$d^2_{13\cdot 24}$	.0541	.4431	−.0003	.2429
$d^2_{14\cdot 23}$	.2647	.0305	.4539	.3389
$B_{12\cdot 34}$	.6647	.7916	1.3164	.3199
$B_{13\cdot 24}$	−.1265	−1.0067	−.2617	−.4812
$B_{14\cdot 23}$	−.4274	−.0553	−3.4805	−.5562
$R^2_{1\cdot 234}$	.7568	.5172	.6575	.5394

SOURCES: See Appendix.

In addition, it is recognized that an $\bar{R}_{1.234}$ of any given size could arise because of chance resulting from sampling variation. Accordingly the customary test of the significance of this value by using a fiducial limit was carried out. In this case the customary 5 per cent level was used. Assuming an $\bar{R}_{1.234}$ of zero (no correlation) in the universe, then if the computed value of $\bar{R}_{1.234}$ is found to be higher than the value which could arise only once in twenty times because of sampling variation, the multiple correlation is deemed to be significant. If an even more rigorous test is desired, then the 1 per cent level of significance can be used; if the computed values for the study still exceed those that could occur only once in a hundred times because of sampling variation, then the correlation can be considered to be significant indeed.

Table XX contains the number of variables used, the number of grouped observations, $R_{1.234}$, $\bar{R}_{1.234}$, and values of R for the 5 per cent and 1 per cent levels of significance.

Table XX

TESTS OF THE SIGNIFICANCE OF THE COMPUTED COEFFICIENTS OF MULTIPLE CORRELATION FOR EACH COMMODITY

Commodity	*Number of Variables*	*Number of Grouped Observations*	$R_{1\cdot234}$	$\bar{R}_{1\cdot234}$	*R for Level of Significance* 5%	1%
Wheat	4	40	.87	.86	.44	.52
Potatoes	4	38	.72	.69	.45	.53
Onions	4	33	.81	.79	.48	.57
Strawberries	4	29	.73	.69	.51	.60

SOURCES: See Appendix.

In every case the $\bar{R}_{1.234}$ values considerably exceeded not only the 5 per cent values for *R* but even the *R* values that would arise just 1 per cent of time because of sampling variation from a statistical universe in which *R* was actually zero. One then can conclude with a comfortable margin of safety that the correlation was highly significant in every case and that the results support the hypothesis.

Adding more independent variables would ultimately bring correlation up toward perfect, as would working with more and more elaborate and complex mathematical relationships. Both of these devices force a fit and also greatly increase the probability of getting a given *R* value (also increasing the *R* value for a given level of significance). In addition, the more complex formulas and the additional variables required to yield perfect correlation for each commodity undoubtedly would not be universal, but rather peculiar and unique to each commodity.

The limited number of variables used, the universality of them, and the simple formula used are offered as the merits of this study. For just these reasons (the simplicity of the formula and the small number of variables) greater significance can be attached to the values computed. All prices exist in a time-space continuum and the correlation using only the basic universal dimensions of mass, time, and space, which are common to both physical and economic phenomena, has yielded coefficients of correlation which can readily be accepted as being significantly high.

The general hypothesis being substantiated, what then of the relationship of price to the individual variables? Was the relationship between price and Gross Economic Population Potential (GEPP) a direct one as was hypothesized? Examination of the sign of $b_{12.34}$ (net regression coefficient showing the effect, in terms of the units used, of GEPP on price with the influence of the other variables removed) in Table XIX reveals the relationship to be a direct one in every case. Similarly the hypothesized inverse relationship between price and both Product Supply Space Potential and Product Supply Time Potential considered independently is supported by an examination of the $b_{13.24}$ and $b_{14.23}$ values in Table XIX. In all the instances these latter two coefficients were found to be negative. The universal effect of an increase in GEPP, other things being equal, was to raise price. The universal effect of an increase in PSSP, other things being equal, was to depress price. The universal effect of an increase in PSTP, other things being equal, was also to depress price.

However, the relative importance of the independent variables might vary considerably from commodity to commodity. The size of the net regression coefficients depend in part upon the units in which the variables are stated. It will be recalled that these measures show the number of units change in price associated with a one unit change in the independent factor, the effect of the other independent variables having been removed statistically. (This statistical removal of effect is the social scientist's approximation of the physical scientist's laboratory methods.)

One method used to estimate the net effect of each independent variable on price is to calculate the d^2 values as indicated in Chapter 3. The squared $R_{1.234}$ is called the coefficient of determination. This $R^2_{1.234}$ value can be split up into components indicating the relative net importance of the particular independent variable with which any one d^2, or coefficient of separate determination as it is called, can be associated.

The values of d^2 in Table XIX indicate that the relative importance of each independent variable does indeed vary from commodity to commodity. Table XIX also contains the values found for β, i.e., the beta coefficient, which, as was explained in Chapter 3, is another measure for estimating the relative net importance of each independent variable separately, this time in terms of the standard deviations of the variables. For reasons indicated subsequently, this beta coefficient is deemed the more reliable of these two measures of individual importance.

To summarize the relative importance of each variable, Table XXI below ranks the d^2 and β values for each commodity with the most important numbered 1 and the least important numbered 3.

Table XXI

RANKINGS OF THE MEASURES OF THE INDIVIDUAL IMPORTANCE OF THE INDEPENDENT VARIABLES FOR EACH COMMODITY MULTIPLE CORRELATION COMPUTED VALUES

Measure of Individual Importance	*Commodity*			
	Wheat	*Potatoes*	*Onions*	*Strawberries*
$d^2_{12\cdot34}$	1	2	2	3
$d^2_{13\cdot24}$	3	1	3	2
$d^2_{14\cdot23}$	2	3	1	1
$B_{12\cdot34}$	1	2	2	3
$B_{13\cdot24}$	3	1	3	2
$B_{14\cdot23}$	2	3	1	1

SOURCES: See Appendix.

In the case of each commodity precisely the same rankings occurred among the two sets of measures. But, in the case of potatoes, whereas both measures seem to indicate that Product Supply Space Potential (PSSP) is clearly the most important factor, the d^2 measure shows Gross Economic Population to be barely more important than Product Supply Time Potential while the β values show it to be much more important.

Considerable caution should be attached to the interpretation of these values for potatoes because it was found that there was a high correlation (.767) between two of the independent variables, i.e., between GEPP and PSSP. (See Part *B* of this chapter.)

In the case of a high correlation between any of the independent variables, the coefficients of separate determination may vary rather erratically and thus be of little use. These separate coefficients are thought to be more subject to random error than the beta coefficients. In addition, each d^2 contains part of the joint determination of the other independent variables.

Although the circumstance of the high correlation of two of the independent variables complicates the problem of separating the effects of the individual variables, it does not negate the significance of the $\overline{R}_{1.234}$ value which measures the collective effect of the independent variables on the dependent one.

Tests of the significance of each of the measures of the individual importance of the independent variables might show the possibility of using only one independent variable to obtain results virtually as good as those obtained by recourse to several variables. This approach to multiple correlation would be first to correlate price with just one independent variable and then add additional variables one at a time, each time computing the coefficient of correlation. The amount of change in the successive coefficients of multiple correlation (and any change can only be an increase since adding more variables cannot lower *R*) could then be tested to see if the change were significant. In this manner those particular independent variables needed to yield the highest significant coefficient of correlation could be found. This entails the concept of the possibility of the increase in *R* being due to sampling variation and hence subject to probability tests concerning the level of significance.

It should be borne in mind that it is not the purpose of this study to analyze the individual peculiarities of the commodities involved. It will be recalled that it is the purpose rather to show that a significantly high *R* can be obtained by recourse to the dimensional analysis set forth in this study and to substantiate the hypotheses concerning the universal effects of the potentials used to express dimensional relationships, thereby furnishing concepts and tools for particular and individual analyses that may be undertaken.

Table XIX does furnish many data for conjecture about individual commodities. For example, Gross Economic Population Potential seems to be quite an important influence on the farm price of wheat; but vast amounts of wheat are raised commercially under conditions of low GEPP. (See Part *B* of this same chapter for a market-production space-association measure indicating this relationship.)

Of course, wheat prices are higher near markets as also are yields on moderately moist lands in contrast to areas far from market with subhumid or semiarid climates, other things being equal. But the beginning student in Economic Geography soon learns that these two circumstances also are associated with land values and the cost of land. Wheat's broader climatic limits, i.e., greater tolerance than many other important crops of dry (and cool) conditions, plus its low perishability and its relatively high value in relation to its bulk, cause certain dry areas far from market to have comparative advantage for the production of wheat. Much regional specialization in wheat production does occur on broad flat plains, sparsely populated, with subhumid or semiarid climate. There an extensive, mechanized, one-crop, commercial system of agriculture prevails.

But, as stated in Part *B* of this chapter, location theory is not being developed, and the locations of production, populations, and incomes are assumed as given for this study although, as also mentioned in Part *B*, a use of potentials in location theory is envisioned.

Apart from the degree of association and the amount of variation "explained" by recourse to the estimating formula, another important matter is the reliability or dependability of the formula for actually estimating a price for a geographical position. The standard error of estimate is a measure of this reliability. The estimated values plus and minus one $S_{1.234}$ establish the range within which lie 68.27 per cent of the actual prices for the commodity involved. The estimated values, plus and minus two standard errors of estimate, establish a range including nearly all the actual prices. The actual figure is 95.46 per cent. (Three standard errors of estimate would include 99.73 per cent.)

Given on p. 92 in Table XXII for each commodity are:

I. The Estimating Equation for each commodity with the computed values substituted for the constants of the general equation used which was:

$$Xc_{1.234} = a_{1.234} + b_{12.34}X_2 + b_{13.24}X_3 + b_{14.23}X_4$$

II. The Standard Error of Estimate.

III. United States Average Farm Price.

The average farm price for each commodity is included merely as a basis for reference for the reader. It must be understood that $S_{1\cdot 234}$ is applied to the computed estimates of price which, of course, vary with the concomitant variation in the known independent variables (in the amounts of the net regression coefficients); once again, then, the caution that the average farm prices are included only as a convenience and for reference only.

Along the same line of reasoning the coefficient of multiple correlation can also be viewed as a measure of the improvement in the estimate of prices (as they vary geographically) that results from using the estimating equation rather than resorting to the average price for

Table XXII

RELIABILITY OF THE ESTIMATES FOR EACH COMMODITY INCLUDING: I—THE ESTIMATING EQUATION, II—STANDARD ERROR OF ESTIMATE ($S_{1\cdot 234}$), AND III—AVERAGE FARM PRICE (INCLUDED AS BASIS FOR REFERENCE ONLY)

Wheat

I. $Xc_{1\cdot 234} = 203.9688 + .5074X_2 - .1705X_3 - 5.3095X_4$

II. \$.04 per bushel

III. \$1.51 per bushel

Potatoes

I. $Xc_{1\cdot 234} = 164.9001 + 1.2651X_2 - .9541X_3 - .1061X_4$

II. \$1.1 per bushel

III. \$1.22 per bushel

Onions

I. $Xc_{1\cdot 234} = 228.9895 + 1.3164X_2 - .2624X_3 - 3.4805X_4$

II. \$.16 per sack (50 lbs. each)

III. \$1.31 per sack (50 lbs. each)

Strawberries

I. $Xc_{1\cdot 234} = 1209.6704 + 3.2057X_2 - 13.5313X_3 - 47.5345X_4$

II. \$.72 per crate (24 quarts each)

III. \$6.36 per crate (24 quarts each)

SOURCES: See Appendix.

the United States as an estimate of the price of the commodity under consideration for all places in the United States.

This raises the whole question of estimates. For want of better data, the arithmetic average alone could have been used. Application of standard deviation would have improved this but still would not result in estimates that varied with other known circumstances. Correlation then "solves" this problem. It permits estimates to be made by utilizing variation in other known variables. This correlation could have been carried out using production by state and population (weighted by income) by state to "explain" price by state. Common sense, supported by inspection of the data, indicates the folly of this. Such a method would overlook the matter of spatial interrelationships among all places and, of course, be unable to handle the problem of the considerable differences in size among the states. Hence a correlation using the concepts of space potential (and those of time also) was developed in this study thereby recognizing, for example, the fact that although Iowa's annual wheat production averaged less than one fourth that of Pennsylvania between 1940 and 1949, the position of Iowa close to the large production in Kansas and the Dakotas caused the supply force influencing Iowa's price to be one and a half times as great as Pennsylvania's as approximated by Wheat Supply Space Potential.

In any event, Table XXII does include average farm price as a convenient reference.

B. *Some Further Applications and Considerations of the Concepts and Techniques Developed*

Utilization of the space potential technique makes possible the measurement of the degree of areal association between certain geographical distributions in cases where such measurement might not otherwise easily be carried out.[1]

Assume, for example, that it is desired that the degree of "market orientation" of the production of a given commodity be measured. That is to say, an attempt is to be made to find the degree of spatial association between the geography of production of a commodity and its geography of consumption.

One method might be to divide a country into a number of subdivisions, as for example into units of, say, 30 miles square. Then the *percentages* of (1) total production and (2) total consumption or some other measure of effective demand could be assigned to each unit. Then a correlation could be run with the resulting coefficient used as a measure of the spatial association of the two factors.

Such a measure has several obvious faults; one of them is technical and the other philosophical. In the first place, the size of the coefficient would vary with the size of the area of the base unit used. Decreasing the size of the unit area lessens the likelihood of spatial association. If the unit area be made small enough, such as could include only the acre on which the crop was raised or the factory producing the gadget, leaving no space for anything else, then the coefficient would be meaningless.

The second objection to a measure so developed is that it does not allow for the fact that limited divisibility of certain factors of production and the consequent economies of large-scale production in certain industries may result in the production of some commodities at a very large scale at a few, sometimes widely separated places,

[1] For a use of population potential as an index of isolation see W. Warntz, "A Methodological Consideration of Some Geographic Aspects of the Newfoundland Referendum on Confederation with Canada, 1948," *The Canadian Geographer*, No. 6 (1955), 39–49.

insofar as transportation costs permit. And further, the production of large amounts at a few widely separated places may represent as high a degree of market-production spatial association as in the case of many small producers located perhaps in such a way as to appear on a dot map to have the same sort of distribution as population also portrayed by a dot map.

It is here submitted that the use of space potential measures helps overcome both of the problems described above.[3]

Both Gross Economic Population Potential (if it be admitted as a measure of accessibility to market) and Product Supply Space Potential (if it be admitted as a measure of the accessibility to the aggregate production of a commodity) could be used for such an analysis since both vary continuously from the spatial standpoint in a space continuum of interrelated distances. They, therefore, are not subjected to the effect of the discontinuity to spatial relationships that the dividing of data into regions, or areas, or units in a grid imposes regardless of whether such a discontinuity be present or not.

Concerning the second suggested difficulty encountered using a unit area method, Supply Space Potentials are measures of proximity to aggregate production at a point regardless of whether that production results from a few areas of very large production or a very large number of areas of small production variously distributed in either case.

Since the two space potentials (demand and supply) have been computed as values for the 48 control points

[3] For a detailed discussion of this problem see W. Warntz, "Measuring Spatial Association With Special Consideration of the Case of Market Orientation of Production," *Journal of the American Statistical Association*, LI (1956).

used to draw the potential maps based on a system of logical contouring, a choice exists as to what points to use to measure the degree of spatial association between the two space potentials. Obviously, it is not just a matter of matching the two sets of contours (although a right-angle crossing would indicate no correlation) for the simple reasons that use of a different contour interval for a map results in the bunching or spreading out of contours and the apparent (but not real) change in "slope". So, it is not just lines on the two maps that are being compared, but rather the spatial coincidence (or lack of it) of the intensities of the two factors and the way they vary geographically. The test cannot be made as it ideally should, at the infinite number of possible geographical points of association, so a certain number needs to be chosen as representative. The alternatives include using evenly spaced points with estimated values for GEPP and PSSP taken from the maps or using 48 "known" values at the control points which are unevenly spaced but are distributed over the whole area. (Of course, the total possible alternatives include also the myriad number of combinations of "known" and estimated values with all degrees of unevenness in spacing.)

But, for the sake of example and simplicity, the values for the 48 state-centered control points were used. It is again pointed out that PSSP could be computed as a "known" value for a control point even though it produced nothing because other producing points contributed to its potential.

These control points were then ranked from lowest value to highest value for each one of the commodity Product Supply Space Potentials in turn. Then, each of these rankings was compared to the ranking of the control points (again lowest to highest) for Gross Economic

Population Potential. The simple formula used to find the association between the ranks was:

$$\rho = 1 - \frac{6 \Sigma d^2}{N (N^2 - 1)}$$

when d equals the difference between the ranks of the two sets of values at a control point and N equals the number of observations; in each case 48.

Rho, i.e., ρ, is interpreted as the coefficient of rank correlation (i.e., straight line to the ranks and, as such, an estimate of a more involved mathematically computed two-variable linear correlation of the actual values). Here, however, this coefficient is given the special name, *Coefficient of Market-Production Spatial Association*, and indicates the over-all degree of market orientation of production of the commodity involved for the entire area under consideration.

Table XXIII contains the ρ values developing out of this particular study.

Table XXIII

COEFFICIENTS OF MARKET PRODUCTION SPATIAL ASSOCIATION

Commodity	ρ
Wheat	−.258
Potatoes	.767
Onions	.395
Strawberries	.587

SOURCES: See Appendix.

Of course these values, once discovered, are surprising to no one knowing the Economic Geography of the United States. Nonetheless, the methodology and the concepts furnish the investigator a means for studying more abstruse circumstances using quantitative data.

However, the discovery of a high degree of market-production spatial association is, of course, the discovery of high correlation between two of the independent variables (X_2 and X_3) used in the analysis of the geographical variation of price. As suggested earlier, this makes more difficult the determination of the net effect of each of these variables separately on price.

Another possible use for potentials would be in the analysis of the change in the geographical variation of the price of a commodity resulting from the addition or the withholding of different amounts of the commodity at various places. Thinking purely in terms of a non-dimensional economics this point might be missed. But, upon reflection one appreciates that the addition of production anywhere adds to potential supply everywhere, by amounts that vary inversely with the distance from the point of injection. Of course, if the amount and/or the point of injection are varied then the resulting contours of Supply Potential would also vary. With these variations there would be differing geographical distributions of price, other things being equal. The universal influence of an increase in supply, other things being equal, is a decrease in price, but the particular effect at a given place, although of course downward, would depend upon the spatial relationship to the point of injection of the new amount. Regional input-output analysis thus might find use for potentials.

Another concept in Economic Geography of considerable importance is *Site and Position.* Site refers to the immediate characteristics or nature of the place in itself, e.g., soil fertility or particular skills of its residing labor force, whereas Position refers to the location of this particular place with regard to other places, e.g., situation with regard to some particular source of raw material.

Gross Economic Population Potential is a measure of the proximity of a point to all income (people weighted by their respective per capita income) as it is geographically distributed. Hence, GEPP can be considered as a measure of the aggregate spatial relationship of the given point to aggregate market, i.e., market accessibility, if effective demand be identified with income or, in the terminology of the Economic Geographer, "Economic-geographic Position" (or even Geonomic Position).

To test the gross relationships between value of an acre of agricultural land and its economic-geographic Position, the following simple study was made. The previously prepared ranking of GEPP was compared with the ranking of the states for average value per acre of their agricultural land in 1950. The coefficient of rank correlation (ρ) indicating the degree of association was found to be .670. This is a gross relationship uncorrected, of course, for Site factors such as differing soil fertility, improvements made on the land (including irrigation facilities in some cases), climatic factors (including the time relationship advantages that may result from being able to produce in the "off season"), and the like. Even so, this coefficient would seem to indicate the importance of Position and spatial relationships.

Iowa's rank was higher in land value than in GEPP, suggesting that its very high soil fertility and desirable climate enhance land values. Conversely, Vermont and West Virginia had higher ranks (considerably so) for GEPP than for value, in all probability because of the limited agricultural yield possibilities inherent in the land itself. Anyone attempting to "explain" agricultural land values or economic rent faces the difficult problem of adequately measuring and then the more difficult problem of combining into an index the complex of Site factor, but GEPP is useful as an approximation of Position. The whole problem of relative time advantage, akin to Time Potential, would also have to be considered. Degree day or development unit measures could be nicely incorporated into the analysis.[3]

This study has outlined in broad general terms certain dimensional relationships in economic phenomena, and has tried to show their relationships to a Geography of Price. The Economic Geographer wishing to carry out further investigation might wish to utilize the estimating formula discovered and work out all the individual estimated prices for each geographic control point and compare them one at a time with the actual prices. He might thereby obtain clues to the differences among parts of the country. If, for example, prices found were consistently higher than the computed ones in the spatial equilibrium for a particular part of the country, this might be a significant fact and its cause might subsequently be found to be due to a price-support program, an artificially adjusted favorable transport rate, or any of a host of man-made artificial factors or peculiar conditions as contrasted to the universal persisting tendencies associated with the dimensions of the phenomena.

It is also recognized that not all units of a commodity are homogeneous as regards quality. This circumstance can complicate an analysis considerably.

Nor would a GEPP map continue to suffice as the map of demand for those commodities for which the demand is derived. Corn, for instance, is used largely as an animal feed to produce meat products; perhaps then the "best" results in an attempt to estimate the geographical variation

[3] For a discussion of degree days and development units, see L. Currie, "Climate and Economic Life," *Geographical Review*, XLII, No. 3 (1952), 367–383.

of the price of corn would be obtained by using a "beef cattle in feed lots" population potential. Derived demand, joint demand (and joint supply), income elasticity of demand, savings, bank credit, and many other topics might be investigated.

Undoubtedly, experimenting with various exponents of distance and also time differences would produce "better" fits.

All these possible improvements would undoubtedly bring about a better approximation of reality which is, of course, inordinately complex, but they would nevertheless be just that—improvements and refinements of the already outlined dimensional analysis using potential values.

If it is argued that using distance (rather than the myriad number of individual and extremely complex actual transport rates) is too great a generalization to be useful, it can also be argued that so using distance factors (in which all units are assumed homogeneous and thereby equally difficult and expensive to overcome) is really assuming an average transport rate for the economy. This logic is, of course, completely in line with the thinking of the Economists who conceive of *an* interest rate for the economy whereas, of course, many, many such rates do actually exist. This average interest rate is used to discount through time and the average transport rate discounts through space. Isard has further suggested[4] that just as there is considered to be "time preference," so might there be considered to exist "space preference." One might even carry the analogy further by suggesting that the matter of "roundaboutness" of production and capital investment, which has been much discussed with

[4] W. Isard, "Distance Inputs and the Space Economy Part I: The Conceptual Framework," *op. cit.*, 193.

regard to time and interest rate, be extended to consider space and transport rate.

It goes almost without saying that other and more complex methods than multiple linear correlation could be employed, using higher powers of each independent variable and, of course, more variables. In this respect only one more variable would seem advisable—Demand Time Potential—because this would add the time dimension to demand and complete the dimensional analysis.

Another important matter that might be considered in further research would be the external forces and factors affecting the American economy. In this study no consideration was made of whether the United States also imported, exported, or did both for a commodity. Consideration of these matters is important and is possible, using potentials for the analysis.

C. Conclusions

This study has been concerned with the Geography of Price. An historical survey of man's considerations of the dimensions of economic and social phenomena, a development of concepts to analyze dimensional influences on price, an actual testing of the hypotheses developed, a consideration of the results of the tests, and finally some suggestions of possible improvements in the concepts and the application of the concepts and techniques of this study to other types of Economic-geographic problems have all been done. There remains then the task of summarizing briefly the conclusions reached in performing the tasks just mentioned.

Although the study has been concerned with geographical variation of price, an appreciation of the necessity of looking at time dimensions and relationships has been cultivated. Therefore, might it not be advisable for those engaged in time series analyses to recognize and take into account the geography of the time data being analyzed?

It is hoped that this study furnishes at least some rudimentary ideas, concepts, and tools whereby the student of spatial distributions can handle time relationships in his analysis. It is further hoped that these concepts also will help the student of time series to handle the spatial aspects of his data, and the scholar who would concern himself with economics as such, the entire dimensions of the phenomena.

This study has taken all the distributions (both time and space) of the raw data as given and has not attempted to explain or account for the patterns. For example, the possible question of whether location of economic activity is price-determined or price-determining or whether both are interrelated and simultaneously determining and determined has not been broached. Rather the other aspect of the space economy, the existence of a spatial price equilibrium, has been investigated. It is conceived that the General Equilibrium Theory of Price which is without dimensions could be expanded to a full dimensional theory by restating the formulas in terms of time and space potentials.

In addition to the price equilibrium aspect of space-economy theory, location theory might incorporate potentials to augment the existing vector analysis which recognizes only certain quantities and distances, rather than interrelated quantities and distances in a space (and time) continuum.

In the last analysis, what then are the conclusions of this study, not expanded by consideration of all the possible refinements and improvements, of more elegant mathematical or statistical techniques, or of the inclusion of particular and specifically limited variables?

Well, it was found that the price of a commodity does indeed tend to vary geographically with the concomitant geographical variation in the intensity of supply and demand. It is also recognized that time relationships should be included in both supply and demand forces to complete the analysis.

Using only the dimensional factors used in this particular study, the hypothesis of the study is stated again, cautiously, but not hesitantly, and this time as a theory (a hypothesis partly verified by fact).

"Price varies from place to place directly with Gross Economic Population Potential and inversely with both Product Supply Space Potential and Product Supply Time Potential."

Stating the theory in terms not peculiar to the terminology of this study only, and recognizing time and space dimensions on both the supply and the demand side, one might make a statement such as the following as an approximation of the Law of Price, useful in accounting for or estimating price variation through time at a given place, or through space at a given time, or for varying combinations of the two.

"Price varies directly with Demand Space Potential and Demand Time Potential and inversely with Product Supply Space Potential and Product Supply Time Potential."

Going even further, one might conceive of the General Equilibrium Price Theory restated in potentials in which all commodity and factor prices are mutually interrelated and simultaneously determining and determined, meaning, then, that all potentials contribute to mutually interrelated and simultaneously determining and determined prices in a time-space continuum.

Appendix

Notes on the Sources of Data for and Construction of Tables and Figures

Tables

Number	*Sources and Methods*
I	U.S.D.A., *Agricultural Statistics*, 1952.
II	U.S.D.C., *Statistical Abstract of the United States*, 1942 through 1952. Data for population from 1940 census and for following years to 1949 from intercensal estimates were averaged arithmetically. Economic Population is an average of Annual Total Income Payments to Individuals for period 1940–1949. Per capita income is a weighted average of annual per capita income payments to individuals during same period.
III	Total of Production from Table I divided into monthly production by use of harvest dates by states from Tables XI, XII, XIII, and XIV, and Production data by states from the same tables.
IV	Created expressly for use in this study.
V	U.S.D.A., *Agricultural Statistics*, 1952.
VI	U.S.D.A., *Agricultural Statistics*, 1952.
VII	U.S.D.C., *Statistical Abstract of the United States*, 1942 through 1952.
VIII	Created expressly for use in this study. Data concerning the geographic center of each of the states in the United States came from U.S.G.S., *U.S. Geological Survey Bulletin 817*, 2nd ed., 1930. Centers given by description in this bulletin — i.e., county, town, bearing, and distance. These centers were then plotted on U.S.D.I. County Map of the United States, 1932 ed., reprinted 1938, scale 1 : 2,500,000, two sheets, Albers equal-area projection (North American datum). Straight-line distances were measured between each state center in turn and all others in 100-mile units to the nearest half. Data were then put into table form, with these tables serving as work sheets.

Number	*Sources and Methods*
IX	Created expressly for use in this study, based on common knowledge.
X	Created expressly for use in this study according to the method outlined in Chapter II from data of Tables VII and VIII.
XI	Production and farm prices from Tables V and VI. Harvest dates compiled from U.S. Bur. of Agr. Ec., *Usual Planting and Harvest Time for Major Field Crops and Commercial Vegetables for Fresh Market by States,* 1948; U.S. Bur. of Agr. Ec., *Commercial Truck Crops for Fresh Market, Usual Planting and Harvesting Dates and Principal Producing Areas by Seasonal Groups and States,* 1951; U.S.D.A., Misc. Pub. 485, *Seedtime and Harvest Time Today,* 1942; U.S. Dept. of Labor, *Major Agricultural Migrant Labor Demand Areas by Month and Principal Crops,* 1950; U.S. Dept. of Labor, *Major Migratory Routes in the Agricultural Labor Market,* 1951; U.S.D.A., *Agricultural Statistics,* 1952.
XII	Production and farm prices from Tables V and VI. Harvest dates compiled from U.S. Bur. of Agr. Ec., *Usual Planting and Harvest Time for Major Field Crops and Commercial Vegetables for Fresh Market by States,* 1948; U.S. Bur. of Agr. Ec., *Commercial Truck Crops for Fresh Market, Usual Planting and Harvesting Dates and Principal Producing Areas by Seasonal Groups and States,* 1951; U.S.D.A., Misc. Pub. 485, *Seedtime and Harvest Time Today,* 1942; U.S. Dept. of Labor, *Major Agricultural Migrant Labor Demand Areas by Month and Principal Crops,* 1950; U.S. Dept. of Labor, *Major Migratory Routes in the Agricultural Labor Market,* 1951; U.S.D.A., *Agricultural Statistics,* 1952.
XIII	Production and farm prices from Tables V and VI. Harvest dates compiled from U.S. Bur. of Agr. Ec., *Usual Planting and Harvest Time for Major Field Crops and Commercial Vegetables for Fresh Market by States,* 1948; U.S. Bur. of Agr. Ec., *Commercial Truck Crops for Fresh Market, Usual Planting and Harvesting Dates and Principal Producing Areas by Seasonal Groups and States,* 1951; U.S.D.A., Misc. Pub. 485, *Seedtime and Harvest Time Today,* 1942; U.S. Dept. of Labor, *Major Agricultural Migrant Labor Demand Areas by Month and Principal Crops,* 1950; U.S. Dept. of Labor, *Major Migratory Routes in*

Number	Sources and Methods
	the Agricultural Labor Market, 1951; U.S.D.A., *Agricultural Statistics,* 1952.
XIV	Production and farm prices from Tables V and VI. Harvest dates compiled from U.S. Bur. of Agr. Ec., *Usual Planting and Harvest Time for Major Field Crops and Commercial Vegetables for Fresh Market by States,* 1948; U.S. Bur. of Agr. Ec., *Commercial Truck Crops for Fresh Market, Usual Planting and Harvesting Dates and Principal Producing Areas by Seasonal Groups and States,* 1951; U.S.D.A., Misc. Pub. 485, *Seedtime and Harvest Time Today,* 1942; U.S. Dept. of Labor, *Major Agricultural Migrant Labor Demand Areas by Month and Principal Crops,* 1950; U.S. Dept. of Labor, *Major Migratory Routes in the Agricultural Labor Market,* 1951; U.S.D.A., *Agricultural Statistics,* 1952.
XV	Created expressly for this study. Supply Space Potential computed according to method outlined in Chapter II from data of Tables VIII and V. GEPP from Table X.
XVI	Created expressly for this study. Supply Space Potential computed according to method outlined in Chapter II from data of Tables VIII and V. GEPP from Table X.
XVII	Created expressly for this study. Supply Space Potential computed according to method outlined in Chapter II from data of Tables VIII and V. GEPP from Table X.
XVIII	Created expressly for this study. Supply Space Potential computed according to method outlined in Chapter II from data of Tables VIII and V. GEPP from Table X.
XIX	Created expressly for this study from data developed by computation.
XX	Created expressly for this study from data developed by computation. Values for levels of significance taken from H. Arkin and R. R. Colton, *Tables for Statisticians,* 1950.
XXI	Created expressly for this study from data developed by computation.
XXII	Created expressly for this study from data developed by computation.
XXIII	Created expressly for this study from data developed by computation.

Figures

Number	*Sources and Methods*
1	Created expressly for this study from data of Tables VIII and IV.
2	Created expressly for this study, using data of Table X and the isogram technique using logical contouring.
3	Created expressly for this study, using data from Table XV and the isogram technique.
4	Created expressly for this study, using data from Table XVI and the isogram technique.
5	Created expressly for this study, based on data from Table XVII and the isogram technique.
6	Created expressly for this study, based on data from Table XVIII and the isogram technique.
7	Created expressly for this study from data in Table XV and a "free-hand" curve.
8	Created expressly for this study, using data from Table XVI and a "free-hand" curve.
9	Created expressly for this study, using data from Table XVII and a "free-hand" curve.
10	Created expressly for this study, using data from Table XVIII and a "free-hand" curve.

Bibliography

Books

Arkin, H., and Colton, R. R. *Tables for Statisticians.* New York: Barnes and Noble, Inc., 1940. Pp. 152.

Carey, H. C. *Principles of Social Science,* 3 vols. Philadelphia: J. B. Lippincott Co., 1858. Pp. 1410.

Chamberlin, E. H. C. *The Theory of Monopolistic Competition.* Cambridge: Harvard University Press, 1933. Pp. 213.

Croxton, F. E., and Cowden, D. J. *Applied General Statistics.* New York: Prentice-Hall, Inc., 1939. Pp. 944.

Dodd, S. C. *Dimensions of Society.* New York: The Macmillan Co., 1942. Pp. 944.

Engländer, O. *Handwörterbuch der Staatswissenschaften,* 4th rev. ed. Jena: G. Fischer, 1926. Pp. 412.

—. *Theorie des Guterverkehrs und der Frachtsätze.* Jena: G. Fischer, 1924. Pp. 202.

Ezekiel, M. *Methods of Correlation Analysis,* 2nd ed. New York: John Wiley and Sons, Inc., 1941. Pp. 531.

Friedrich, C. J. *Alfred Weber's Theory of the Location of Industries.* Chicago: University of Chicago Press, 1929. Pp. 256.

Gray, A. *The Development of Economic Doctrine.* London: Longmans, Green and Co., 1931. Pp. 384.

Hoover, E. M. *The Location of Economic Activity.* New York: McGraw-Hill Book Company, Inc., 1948. Pp. 310.

Lösch, A. *Die Räumliche Ordnung der Wirtschaft.* Jena: G. Fischer, 1940. Pp. 348.

Martineau, H. *The Philosophy of Auguste Comte.* London: Trübner and Company, 1853. Pp. 838.

Mendeleyev, D. I. *K. Poznaniyu Rossii* (Information on Russia). St. Petersburg: A. S. Suvorina Publishing House, 1906. Pp. 157.

Mill, J. S. *Principles of Political Economy,* 2 vols. London: J. W. Parker and Son, 1848. Pp. 1013.

Moore, J. H. *Handbook of Financial Mathematics.* New York: Prentice-Hall, Inc., 1940. Pp. 1216.

Moroney, M. J. *Facts from Figures*. Harmondworth, Middlesex: Penguin Books, Ltd., 1951. Pp. 472.

Palander, T. *Beiträge Zur Standortstheorie*. Uppsala: Almqvist and Wiksells Boktrycheri—A.B., 1935. Pp. 419.

Quetelet, A. *Sur l'homme*. Brussels: Haman and Company, 1836. Pp. 323.

Rink, F. T. (ed.). *Immanuel Kant's Physische Geographie*. Königsberg: Nicolovius, 1802. Pp. 568.

Thünen, J. von. *Der Isolierte Staat in Beziehung auf Landwirtschaft und Nationalökonomie*, 3 vols. Hamburg and Rostock: 1836–1863. Pp. 678.

Walras, L. *Elements d'economie Politique pure, ou Theorie de la Richesse Social*. Lausanne: Paris and Bale, 1874. Pp. 208.

Weber, A. *Über den Standort der Industrien*. Tubingen: 1909. Pp. 512.

Weigmann, H. *Kritischer Beitrag zur Theorie des International en Handels*. Jena: G. Fischer, 1926. Pp. 316.

—. *Politische Raumsordnung*. Hamburg: Hanseatische Verlagsanstalt, 1935. Pp. 50.

Zipf, G. K. *Human Behavior and the Principle of Least Effort*. Cambridge: Addison-Wesley Press, 1949. Pp. 573.

Articles

Abrams, R. H. "Residential Propinquity as a Factor in Marriage Selection," *American Sociological Review*, VIII (1943), 288–294.

Bortkiewicz, F. "Letter," *Deutsche Literaturzeitung*, XXXI (1910), 1717–1724.

Bossard, J. H. S. "Residential Propinquity as a Factor in Marriage Selection," *American Journal of Sociology*, XXXVIII (1932), 219–224.

Curie, L. "Climate and Economic Life," *Geographical Review*, XLII, No. 3 (1952), 367–383.

Davie, M. R., and Reeves, R. J. "Propinquity of Residence Before Marriage," *Americal Journal of Sociology*, XLIV (1939), 510–517.

Dodd, S. C. "Scientific Methods in Human Relations," *The American Journal of Economics and Sociology*, X, No. 3 (1950), 221–235.

Engländer, O. "Kirtisches und Positives zu einer allgemeiner reinen Lehre vom Standort," *Zeitschrift fur Volkswirtschaft und Sozialpolitik*, V, Nos. 7–9 (1926), Pp. 306.

Furlan, V. "Die Standortsprobleme un der Volks-und Weltwirtschaftslehre," *Weltwirtschaftliches Archiv*, II (1913), 1–34.

Hartshorne, R. "The Nature of Geography," *Annals of the Association of American Geographers*, XXIX, Nos. 3 and 4 (1939), Pp. 482.

Hilgard, J. E. "The Advance of Population in the United States," *Scribner's Monthly*, IV (1872), 214.

Isard, W. "Distance Inputs and the Space-Economy. Part I: The Conceptual Framework," *The Quarterly Journal of Economics*, LXV (1951), 181–198.

—. "The General Theory of Location and Space-Economy," *Quarterly Journal of Economics*, LXIII (1949), 476–506.

—. "Interregional and Regional Input-Output Analysis: A Model of a Space-Economy," *The Review of Economics and Statistics*, XXXIII, No. 4 (1951), 318–328.

Isbell, E. "Internal Migration in Sweden and Intervening Opportunities," *American Sociological Review*, IX (1944), 627–639.

Launhardt, W. "Die Bestimmung des zweckmässigsten Standortes einer gewerblicken Anlage," *Zeitschrift des Vereins deutscher Ingenieure*, XXVI, No. 3 (1882), 67–85.

Lösch, A. "Beitrage zur Standortstheorie," *Schmollers Jahrbuch*, LXII (1938), 329–335.

Predöhl, A. "Das Standortsproblem in der Wirtschaftstheorie," *Weltwirtschaftliches Archiv*, XXI (1925), 294–331.

—. "The Theory of Location in its Relation to General Economics," *Journal of Political Economy*, XXXVI (1928), 370–391.

Ravenstein, E. G. "The Laws of Migration," *Journal of the Royal Statistical Society* (1885), 167–227.

Ritschl, H. "Reine und historische Dynamik des Standortes des Erzengungsweige," *Schmollers Jahrbuch*, LI (1927), 813–870.

Schumpeter, J. "Letter," *Jahrbuch für Gesetzgebung, Verwaltung und Volkswirtschaft*, XXXIV, No. 3 (1910), 444–447.

Stewart, J. Q. "A Basis for Social Physics," *Impact*, II, No. 2 (1952), 110–133.

—. "Concerning Social Physics," *Scientific American*, CLXXVIII (1948), 20–23.

—. "Demographic Gravitation: Evidence and Applications," *Sociometry*, XI, Nos. 1–2 (1948), 31–58.

—. "The Development of Social Physics," *American Journal of Physics*, XVIII, No. 5 (1950), 239–243.

—. "Empirical Mathematical Rules Concerning the Distribution and Equilibrium of Population," *The Geographical Review*, XXXVII (1947), 461–485.

Stewart. J. Q. "Potential of Population and its Relationship to Marketing," *Theory in Marketing*. Edited by R. Cox and W. Alderson. Chicago: Richard D. Irwin, Inc., 1950. Pp. 19–40.

Stouffer, S. A. "Intervening Opportunities: A Theory Relating Mobility and Distance," *American Sociological Review*, V (1940), 845–867.

Thomas, D. S. "Interstate Migration and Intervening Opportunities," *American Sociological Review*, VI (1941), 773–783.

Weigmann, H. "Ideen zu einer Theorie der Raumwirtschaft," *Weltwirtschaftliches Archiv*, XXXIV (1931), 1–40.

—. "Standortstheorie und Raumwirtschaft," *Joh. Heinr. von Thünen zum 150 Geburstag*. Edited by W. Seedorf and H. Jurgen. Rostock: Carl Hinstorffs, 1933. Pp. 137–157.

Wright, J. K. "Some Measures of Distribution," *Annals of the Association of American Geographers*, XXVII, No. 4 (1937), 177–212.

Zipf, G. K. "The Hypothesis of the 'Minimum Equation' as a Unifying Social Principle: With Attempted Synthesis," *American Sociological Review*, XII (1947), 627–650.

Public Documents

Douglas, E. M. *Boundaries, Areas, Geographic Centers and Altitudes of the United States and the Several States* (Bulletin No. 817), Washington: United States Geological Survey, 1930. Pp. 265.

Hainsworth, R. G., Baker, O. E., and Brodell, A. P. *Seed Time and Harvest Today* (Miscellaneous Publication No. 485), Washington: United States Department of Agriculture, 1942. Pp. 97.

United States Bureau of Agricultural Economics. *Commercial Truck Crops for Fresh Markets, Usual Planting and Harvesting Dates, and Principal Producing Areas by Seasonal Groups and States*, Washington: United States Department of Agriculture, 1951. Pp. 89.

United States Bureau of Agricultural Economics. *Usual Planting and Harvest Time for Major Field Crops and for Commercial Vegetables for Fresh Markets by States*, Washington: United States Department of Agriculture, 1948. Pp. 150.

United States Department of Agriculture. *Agricultural Statistics*, 1952, Washington: Government Printing Office, 1952. Pp. 876.

United States Department of Commerce. *Statistical Abstract of the United States*, Editions 63–73, Washington: Government Printing Office, 1942–1952. Pp. 1000 each.

United States Department of the Interior. *United States County Map*,

2 sheets (Albers Equal-Area Projection; North American Datum; Scale—1/2,500,000) Washington: 1932.

United States Farm Placement Service. *Major Agricultural Migrant Labor Demand Areas*, Washington: United States Department of Labor, 1950, Pp. 12.

United States Farm Placement Service. *Major Migratory Routes in the Agricultural Labor Market* (Map), Washington: United States Department of Labor, 1951.

Index

www.ingramcontent.com/pod-product-compliance
Lightning Source LLC
La Vergne TN
LVHW010319220926
848484LV00004BB/790

Just Like That, Your Life Changed. What Now?

Here are 15 Key Steps to Heal and Live Again After a Loss

If you've recently experienced the devastating loss of a spouse, parent, sibling, friend, or even a beloved pet, you may feel blindsided, numb, overwhelmed, and mentally stuck. Life becomes mechanical. You handle what's urgent, and nothing more. You wonder if you'll ever feel like yourself again.

In her book, *Your Amazing Itty Bitty™ Grief Journey 101,* Dr. Kimberly Q. Hubenette gently walks you from survival mode to one of strength. With compassion, clarity, and practical wisdom, she guides you through the stages of grief, from emotional emergency to renewed purpose, offering real tools for real healing.

Inside this powerful book, you'll discover how to:

- Reclaim your physical and emotional health
- Set boundaries with negative people
- Rediscover meaning and purpose
- Get out and start living your new life with courage
- And so much more

If you're ready to begin healing after devastating loss and take your first brave steps toward a new way of living, pick up a copy of this must-read Itty Bitty™ Book today!